LENSES ON LEARNING
MODULE 3

Observing Today's Mathematics Classroom

Readings

Edited by
Catherine Miles Grant, Barbara Scott Nelson, Ellen Davidson,
Annette Sassi, Amy Shulman Weinberg, Jessica Bleiman

Center for the Development of Teaching
Education Development Center
Newton, Massachusetts

DALE SEYMOUR PUBLICATIONS
Pearson Learning Group

National Science Foundation

This work was supported by the National Science Foundation under Grant No. ESI-9731242 and by The Pew Charitable Trusts. Any opinions, findings, conclusions, or recommendations expressed here are those of the authors and do not necessarily reflect the views of these organizations.

Special thanks are due to our editor, Beverly Cory. Her understanding of the ideas in these materials and their pedagogical stance, coupled with her commitment to clarity, made the materials much more understandable and usable.

Art and Design: Senja Lauderdale, Jim O'Shea, April Okano

Editorial: Doris Hirschhorn

Manufacturing: Mark Cirillo, Sonia Pap

Marketing: Douglas Falk

Production: Karen Edmonds, Alia Lesser

Publishing Operations: Carolyn Coyle, Tom Daning, Richetta Lobban

ISBN 0-7690-3032-7

Printed in the United States of America

1 2 3 4 5 6 7 8 9 10 07 06 05 04 03 02

1-800-321-3106
www.pearsonlearning.com

The *Lenses on Learning* Project

Project Staff, Education Development Center

Barbara Scott Nelson (PI)

Jessica Bleiman

Ellen Davidson

Catherine Miles Grant

Annette Sassi

Amy Shulman Weinberg

Sheila Flood

Pilot-Test Facilitators

Jeffrey Benson
Principal and Director of Educational Services
Germaine Lawrence School
Arlington, Massachusetts

Valerie Gumes
Principal, Blue Hills Early Education Center
Boston, Massachusetts

Joanne Gurry
Assistant Superintendent, Arlington
Public Schools
Arlington, Massachusetts

Eric Johnson
Principal, Dever School
Boston, Massachusetts

Joseph Petner
Principal, Haggerty School
Cambridge, Massachusetts

Emily Shamieh
Principal, Winthrop School
Boston, Massachusetts

Debra Shein-Gerson
Elementary Mathematics Curriculum Coordinator
Brookline, Massachusetts

Casel Walker
Principal, Manning School
Boston, Massachusetts

These pilot tests took place in eastern Massachusetts under the auspices of the Boston Public Schools, Education Collaborative of Greater Boston (EDCO); Lesley College; and the Merrimack Education Center.

Field-Test Sites

Albuquerque Public Schools
Albuquerque, New Mexico

Clark County School District
Las Vegas, Nevada

Durham Public Schools
Durham, North Carolina

Greenville County Public Schools
Greenville, South Carolina

Mt. Holyoke College
South Hadley, Massachusetts

Madison Elementary School District #38
Phoenix, Arizona

SUNY-Cortland
Cortland, New York

University of Washington
Seattle, Washington

Project Evaluators, Education Development Center

Barbara Miller

Michael Foster

Sarah Gray

Project Advisors

Diane Briars
Pittsburgh Public Schools

Nancy Dickerson
Boston Public Schools

Judy Mumme
Mathematics Renaissance K–12

Joseph Murphy
The Ohio State University

Mildred Collins Pierce
Harvard Graduate School of Education

Susan Jo Russell
TERC, Cambridge, Massachusetts

James Spillane
Northwestern University

Virginia Stimpson
University of Washington

Philip Wagreich and Kathy Kelso
University of Illinois at Chicago

CONTENTS

INTRODUCTION

Many schools today are engaged in the work of aligning the teaching and learning of mathematics to NCTM's *Principles and Standards for School Mathematics* (2000), one of a series of publications dedicated to improving mathematics instruction nationwide. Administrators in these schools are looking for ways they can reflect on and support the changes that are taking place. You may now, or at some time in the future, find yourself sharing their interest.

No administrative functions are more central to a high-quality instructional program than classroom observation and teacher supervision. If you are like most of today's administrators, you have been trained to use classroom observations and the post-observation conference to evaluate and report on a teacher's capacity to implement teaching techniques and behaviors believed to be applicable across grade levels and subject matter. Increasingly, though, research showing that children's learning is subject-specific has led supervisors to consider content-specific principles and methods of teaching as well. At the same time, the role of supervisor as expert advisor is expanding to include working collaboratively with teachers to consider the nature of the mathematical thinking of the children in the class and the instruction underway. Although evaluation of teachers continues to be important, increasing attention is being paid to promoting teacher development and building a professional community among the diversity of teachers in schools.

Changes in mathematics education combined with changes in the field of supervision point to the need for you, as an administrator, to think carefully about the purpose and process of supervising teachers. In particular, you need to consider the ways in which you can be helpful to teachers as a mentor. These developments suggest that you do the following:

1. Realize that teachers are sometimes struggling as they construct their own understandings about mathematics learning and teaching

2. Develop collaborative relationships with teachers, working with them to make sense of the learning and teaching opportunities that arise in their own classrooms and in their school community

3. Move away from a reliance on hierarchical authority and instead regard supervision as part of a democratic and professional process

4. Recognize that teachers' unique backgrounds influence their pedagogy and their approaches to supervision

5. Develop a more finely tuned professional judgment about teaching and learning in the classroom, especially within the various disciplines

The nuances of classroom practice are both subtle and significant, and they lie at the very heart of these changes.

This *Lenses on Learning* module helps you develop an "eye" for the nuances of standards-based instructional practice so that you can make more informed judgments about the quality of the instruction that you observe. You are encouraged to look beyond the surface features of a classroom—the curriculum itself and the teaching strategies—to discern the nature of the intellectual activity that is unfolding within.

The classrooms in which teachers are working to align with the NCTM *Standards* can look very different from the elementary arithmetic class of 10 or 20 years ago. The flow of the lessons feels different: Class may begin with students working together in small groups, talking freely among themselves while the teacher circulates to ask questions, make suggestions, or assist students; later, everyone joins in a whole-group discussion. The discourse in the classroom may sound very different: Students talk with and to each other, explaining strategies, asking each other questions, raising points of disagreement.

Making sense of such classrooms and the learning that is going on can be challenging if you did not learn or teach mathematics in this way yourself. From your frame of reference, these classrooms may seem disorganized, chaotic, or unfocused. You might wonder what the topic of the lesson is, whether the teacher has a long-range mathematical agenda or immediate learning objectives, and whether students are even understanding the material. The teacher may confound your expectations about exercising authority in the classroom. One goal for *Lenses on Learning, Module 3* is to help you grow accustomed to the look, the sound, and the feel of classrooms that are moving toward standards-based practice.

Yet, being comfortable with the instructional flow in such classrooms is only the beginning. The observable differences in classroom organization and instructional practice reflect fundamentally different notions of what knowledge is and what it means to learn and teach. An equally important goal of this module, then, is to help you discern the mathematical content of a teacher's lesson, the nature of the students' ideas about that content, and the ways the teacher helps students deepen their understanding of those ideas.

Threaded through each session of this module are three experiences for the participants of this course:

◆ **You will develop an eye for standards-based classrooms.** Effective teacher supervision depends on being able to dig beneath the surface features of a classroom to see the mathematical ideas that are at play and the thinking and learning that are taking place. You will need to understand the nature of those mathematical ideas and the structure of lessons that help all learners develop rich and complex understandings of these ideas over time. With this new "eye," you can be more discerning about the use of pedagogical practices—as well as instructional tools and technologies—and how they advance the learning.

◆ **You will come to understand what a teacher's long-term mathematical agenda might be and the role of such an agenda in teaching.** When a teacher's vision is focused on the mathematical ideas that students need to develop, that teacher brings a long-range perspective to the on-the-spot dilemmas and decisions of daily classroom life. A long-term mathematical agenda is not a list of topics to be covered that year—division, fractions, and so forth; nor is it a list of skills that students should attain, such as "two-digit subtraction with regrouping." Rather, a teacher's long-term mathematical agenda comprises that relatively small set of fundamental mathematical ideas and ways of thinking that are the goal of the teacher's instruction for the year. The long-term agenda at third grade, for example, might include understanding that multiplication is about combining groups of things and developing several ways of doing this. A mathematical agenda helps the teacher navigate the myriad choices that arise in any given lesson. As students' ideas and confusions present themselves, awareness of the long-term agenda helps a teacher decide which of these to pursue.

◆ **You will begin to rethink your supervisory relationship with teachers.** New perceptions of your role can release you from the obligation to "move teachers" by dispensing expert advice and open the door to your becoming a collaborative inquirer with the teachers in your district.

In this seminar, you explore the topics in a variety of modes: through readings, by examining students' mathematical work as depicted on videotape, and by watching teachers on videotape who are in the process of reforming their instructional practice. You and the other administrators in your *Lenses on Learning* class will function as a reflective community, thinking through and talking together about the ideas that emerge from the readings, videotapes, and teacher and student work.

The four readings in this book constitute part of your work for *Lenses on Learning, Module 3: Observing Today's Mathematics Classroom.* Assignments from this book will be made as you proceed through the class sessions. Additionally, you may find that some of these readings, as well as the materials described in the Resource List at the end of the book, are valuable references to share with members of your school community: teachers, parents, and school boards.

The Impact of Today's Mathematics on Your Supervisory Role

The *Lenses on Learning* course as a whole offers an introduction to the ideas about mathematics learning and teaching that are evident in classrooms aligned with the NCTM *Standards. Lenses on Learning, Module 3* focuses on the implications of such ideas for the areas of classroom observation and teacher supervision.

To prepare for the first session of *Observing Today's Mathematics Classroom,* please read the following:

READING 1   "Changing Perspectives in Curriculum and Instruction"
(Nolan and Francis)

As you read, mark those paragraphs or short sections that seem most salient. Be prepared to discuss with other course participants why you think these passages are significant. In particular, be prepared to discuss the following question:

◆   What strikes you about Nolan and Francis's view of the impact of current theories of learning and teaching on supervision practices? Why?

Although this reading will be explicitly discussed in Session 1, keep in mind that it has implications for your work throughout the entire module.

Changing Perspectives in Curriculum and Instruction

James Nolan and Pam Francis

This chapter considers the potential impact of contemporary theories of learning and teaching on supervisory practice. Although theorists usually conceive of curriculum and instruction as separate entities, we have chosen not to consider the two separately in this chapter. Curriculum and instruction are frequently separated for purposes of discussion and analysis of the educational process; but in the learning-teaching act, decisions about what to teach (i.e., curriculum) and how to teach it (i.e., instruction) must be reconciled and unified. It is in the learning-teaching act that supervision finds its focus and direction.

Educational practices—and indeed all of human behavior—are guided largely by what Sergiovanni (1985) has termed *mindscapes*. Mindscapes are mental frameworks or paradigms through which we envision reality and our place in reality. They are usually more implicit and unexamined than explicit. As such, mindscapes are taken for granted and provide a set of beliefs or assumptions that exert a tremendous influence on behavior. Sergiovanni states:

> Mindscapes provide us with intellectual and psychological images of the real world and the boundaries and parameters of rationality that help us to make sense of the world. In a very special way, mindscapes are intellectual security blankets on the one hand, and road maps through an uncertain world on the other (Sergiovanni 1985, p. 5).

The major thesis of this chapter is that the mindscapes that currently drive both supervision theory and practice will undergo significant alteration as a result of important changes in educators' conceptions of learning and teaching that have evolved during the 1980s. We have developed this thesis through a three-part structure: (1) an examination of traditional views of the learning-teaching process, (2) an examination of changing perspectives on the learning-teaching process, and

AUTHOR NOTE: We are grateful to Bernard Badiali, J. Robert Coldiron, and Lee Goldsberry for comments on earlier versions of this chapter.

(3) an examination of the implications of these changing perspectives for the practice of supervision.

Traditional Views of Learning and Teaching

The traditional view of the learning-teaching process, which has dominated instruction in most schools, can be captured in five fundamental beliefs about learning. The power of these beliefs rests not in any particular one, but rather in the fact that they constitute a mutually reinforcing system of beliefs. Even though these beliefs are very powerful in driving much of what we currently do in the name of educational practice, for most educators they have remained largely implicit and unexamined. In fact, we derived our descriptions of these beliefs from an analysis of what schools and educators actually do as they attempt to educate learners, rather than from an analysis of what schools and educators espouse. These five fundamental beliefs are:

1. Learning is the process of accumulating bits of information and isolated skills.

2. The teacher's primary responsibility is to transfer his knowledge directly to students.

3. Changing student behavior is the teacher's primary goal.

4. The process of learning and teaching focuses primarily on the interactions between the teacher and individual students.

5. Thinking and learning skills are viewed as transferable across all content areas.

These five beliefs have important implications for teaching. Given these beliefs, the most important teaching tasks are the following:

- Organizing and structuring the learning material in the most appropriate sequence.

- Explaining concepts clearly and unambiguously.

- Using examples and illustrations that can be understood by students.

- Modeling appropriate application of desired skills.

- Checking student comprehension of the material that has been presented.

- Structuring and organizing practice sessions with instructional material so that it will be retained more effectively in long-term memory and transferred appropriately to other contexts.

- Assessing student learning by requiring students to reproduce the desired knowledge and skills on paper-and-pencil tests or through other observable means.

These beliefs have resulted in a teacher-centered conception of teaching and supervision in which the teacher's observable behavior during instruction occupies the center stage of the educational drama. The supervisor works one-to-one with each teacher in a two-step process: (1) the supervisor uses paper-and-pencil observation instruments to carefully capture and document the teacher's observable behavior during instruction; and (2) the supervisor and teacher come together in a conference designed primarily to relate the teacher's observable behavior to both individual student behavior and to research findings on generalizable teaching behaviors that seem to be effective in promoting student learning.

Changing Perspectives on Learning and Teaching

During the 1980s, the shape of educational practice slowly began to change, creating a new mindscape about human learning. This new framework has the potential not only to change teaching behavior on a large-scale basis, but also to cause us to fundamentally alter our beliefs about supervision. This new mindscape, or view of learning and teaching, can also be encapsulated in several interrelated beliefs about the nature of learning and teaching. Some of these beliefs are based on theories of learning that are relatively new; others are based on theories of learning that have existed for many years but have exerted little influence on practice.

1. *All learning, except for simple rote memorization, requires the learner to actively construct meaning.* Learners construct meaning by taking new information, relating it to their prior knowledge, and then putting their new understandings to use in reasoning and problem solving. "In this process, each person is continuously checking new information against old rules, revising the old rules when discrepancies appear and reaching new understandings or constructions of reality" (Brooks 1990, p. 68). For learning to occur, the learner must actively engage in the mental processes necessary to construct the new meanings and understandings. Although learning theorists have held this belief for many years (see Dewey 1902), only recently have concerted efforts been made to help practitioners put this notion into practice (see Lampert 1990).

2. *Students' prior understandings of and thoughts about a topic or concept before instruction exert a tremendous influence on what they learn during instruction.*

> What people learn is never a direct replica of what they have read or been told or even of what they have been drilled on. We know that to understand something is to interpret it and further that an interpretation is based partly on what we've been told or have read but also on what we already know and on general reasoning and logical abilities (Brandt 1988–89, p. 15).

One of the teacher's most important tasks must be to explore the conceptions that learners bring with them to the classroom and help them achieve a new, more refined understanding of those concepts. When learners' preexisting conceptions are inaccurate, the teacher must provide experiences that assist the learners to recognize the inaccuracies. Otherwise, their misconceptions are not likely to change as a result of instruction. "It is not sufficient to simply present students with the correct facts. One has to change the concepts or schemas that generated the inaccurate beliefs" (Bransford and Vye 1989, p. 188).

3. *The teacher's primary goal is to generate a change in the learner's cognitive structure or way of viewing and organizing the world.* The most important factor in any learning-teaching situation is not the observable behavior of either the teacher or the learner. The single most important factor in determining how much a

student learns during instruction is the learner's cognitive processing of information during instruction (Anderson 1989). Changes in observable behavior are important because they can be used to infer that the learner's cognitive structure has changed, but changes in behavior are an indicator of learning and a result of learning, not the learning itself.

4. *Because learning is a process of active construction by the learner, the teacher cannot do the work of the learning.* Students must do the work of learning (Schlechty 1990). The teacher's task is to help learners acquire the skills and dispositions needed to carry out the work of learning. This means: (a) helping learners acquire learning and thinking strategies; (b) helping learners acquire the metacognitive understanding needed to choose the appropriate learning strategy for a given instructional task and to self-monitor the use of the strategy; and (c) motivating learners to engage in appropriate thinking during instruction. The teacher moves from the role of protagonist to that of director or drama coach, and the student becomes the main character in the educational drama.

5. *Learning in cooperation with others is an important source of motivation, support, modeling, and coaching.* In contrast to the traditional view of learning as a solitary process, the new mindscape recognizes the important role that peers can play in the learning process by sharing responsibility for the learning of all group members. Most successful instructional programs designed to teach higher order cognitive skills prescribe the use of cooperative learning groups focused on meaning-construction activities. Such activities provide a type of cognitive apprenticeship in which students have multiple opportunities to observe others do the work that they are expected to do (Resnick and Klopfer 1989). There is ample evidence that when students are engaged in cooperative learning activities that are structured to include both group interdependence and individual accountability, they learn more (Slavin 1989–90).

6. *Content-specific learning and thinking strategies play a much more important role in learning than was previously recognized.* Until the past decade, much of the research on learning focused on learning strategies and skills that were general in nature and applied across subject matter. "One of the great luxuries of the old style research on learning was that you could look for principles that had general validity. Now we believe that we must first immerse ourselves in the study of how people learn particular things in particular environments" (Brandt 1988–89, p. 14). In the past few years, the pendulum has swung from an exclusive emphasis on general thinking and learning skills to an increasing emphasis on content-specific learning and thinking skills. Perkins and Salomon (1989) agree with the contention that content-specific learning skills were neglected by educational researchers for a long period of time and suggest that learning and thinking skills are most likely a synthesis of general cognitive strategies and context or content-specific techniques.

As was true for research on learning, process-product research on teaching (which provides the basis for much of our current work in supervision and staff development) has focused almost exclusively on teaching techniques that are applicable across grade levels and subject matter. This heavy emphasis on general principles and methods of teaching to the exclusion of content-specific principles and methods has come under fire from a number of educational researchers in recent years.

One content specialist, Henry (1986), argues that the field of instructional supervision and its emphasis on general notions of teaching has violated the field of English education through the institutionalization of behaviorist views of learning and teaching. Henry paints a picture of thousands of English teachers scurrying to write behavioral objectives, create improved feedback and management loops, and use mastery learning strategies. He sees these activities as antithetical to the very nature of English.

> What is neglected or generally omitted is the fundamental probing of instruction which lies not solely in overt, externally observable behavior but also in the internalized arrangement of ideas most of which are predetermined by the discipline. Time is different in history, in physics, in biology, in mathematics, and in English (Henry 1986, p. 20).

Henry's views concerning the importance of content-specific conceptions of learning and teaching have been well supported in recent years by the work of several teacher educators, such as Buchman (1984).

> Curriculum practices and development in many schools and colleges of education can be interpreted as a flight away from content. Teachers without content are like actors without scripts. Teaching is conditional on the presence of educational content and essential activities of teaching are conditional upon the content knowledge of teachers (pp. 29–30).

The importance of content knowledge in the teaching process has also been the primary focus of study of Shulman and his associates. They have identified general pedagogical knowledge, subject matter knowledge, and pedagogical content knowledge as critical components of the professional knowledge base in teaching (Wilson, Shulman, and Richert 1987). Pedagogical content knowledge is a relatively new and illuminating construct that refers to the "capacity of a teacher to transform the content knowledge he or she possesses into forms that are pedagogically powerful and yet adaptive to the variations in ability and background presented by the students" (Shulman 1987, p. 15). Included among the various aspects of pedagogical content knowledge are: (1) the teacher's view of how the discipline should be represented to students, (2) the teacher's understanding of how easy or difficult particular concepts will be for specific groups of students to learn, and (3) the teacher's possession of a variety of examples, metaphors, analogies, and narratives that can be used to make the concepts in the discipline more understandable for students. Wilson, Shulman, and Richert (1987) see the teacher's pedagogical content knowledge as a critical attribute in the process of preparing for, delivering, and reflecting on instruction.

In short, to paraphrase Shulman (1990), when the content to be taught becomes a starting point for the process of inquiry and researchers begin to ask what is good teaching of mathematics or what is good teaching of *Romeo and Juliet,* the answers and related questions seem to be quite different from the answers received when one begins by asking what is good teaching in general.

These six beliefs, which characterize the changing mindscape on learning and teaching, call into serious question the portrait that we painted earlier of the supervisor who works one-on-one with each teacher to document observable behavior and move that behavior into greater alignment with the research on general teaching effectiveness. Indeed, the new mindscape on learning and teaching demands a significantly altered mindscape on supervision.

Implications for Supervision

The changing perspectives on learning and teaching have five important implications:

1. Teachers should be viewed as active constructors of their own knowledge about learning and teaching.

2. Supervisors should be viewed as collaborators in creating knowledge about learning and teaching.

3. The emphasis on data collection during supervision should change from almost total reliance on paper-and-pencil observation instruments to capture the events of a single period of instruction to the use of a variety of data sources to capture a lesson as it unfolds over several periods of instruction.

4. Both general principles and methods of teaching as well as content-specific principles and methods of teaching should be attended to during the supervisory process.

5. Supervision should become more group oriented rather than individually oriented.

Teachers as Active Knowledge Constructors

Just as students must actively construct new knowledge, teachers must be active participants in constructing their own knowledge. The mindscape that has been dominant in supervision has viewed supervision and staff development as vehicles for training teachers to adopt practices and to use knowledge that has been produced by others, principally by researchers on teaching. Just as it is impossible for teachers to pour their knowledge into the heads of students, it is equally impossible for supervisors and staff developers to pour the knowledge and practices recommended by researchers into the heads of teachers. Teachers who choose to adopt new practices are not empty vessels to be filled with someone else's ideas. They are learners who are re-educating themselves to become experts in another mode of teaching (Putnam 1990). Much of our knowledge about learning remains unused in classrooms not because teachers are unwilling to use it, but because they have not been given the opportunity and the time to work with the concepts and practices in order to relate them to their own knowledge, experience, and contexts—to truly make them their own. Before teachers can use a new model of teaching effectively, they must acquire a deep, personalized understanding of the model. Support for this statement can be derived from the work of Joyce and Showers (1988), which demonstrates that at least thirty to forty hours of study, practice, and feedback are required before teachers gain executive control over complex teaching models. Executive control means that the trainer can use the model well technically, can distinguish between appropriate and inappropriate opportunities for applying the model, and can adapt the model to particular students and contexts.

Perhaps most important, teachers must be looked on as generators of knowledge on learning and teaching, not merely as consumers of research. "What is missing from the knowledge base for teaching, therefore, are the voices of teachers themselves, the questions teachers ask, the way teachers use writing and intentional talk in their work lives, and the interpretive frames teachers use to understand and improve their own classroom practice" (Cochran-Smith and Lytle 1990, p. 2).

When driven by the new mindscapes on learning and teaching, supervision becomes a vehicle for inquiry and experimentation—aimed at knowledge generation, not simply knowledge adoption. The primary purpose of supervision becomes *the improvement of teaching and learning by helping teachers acquire a deeper understanding of the learning-teaching process.* Knowledge generation can be achieved when supervision becomes a process of action research in which the supervisor and the teacher use classroom learning and teaching activities as a vehicle for testing their own ideas, ideas and practices of colleagues, and findings derived from more formal research studies in terms of their application to the unique educational context in which the teacher and supervisor function.

This view of supervision has been advocated quite powerfully by Schön (1989) and Garman (1986). Garman has taken the view of clinical supervision espoused by Cogan (1973), one of the originators of clinical supervision, and expanded it to be more compatible with current perspectives on learning and teaching. Cogan's model of supervision was grounded in the traditional views of learning, which saw the teacher as the adopter of practices that had been shown as effective through the work of researchers and developers. He did not envision teachers as researchers (Garman 1986). Garman, on the other hand, points out the necessity for clinical supervisors to engage teachers in the process of self-supervision through reflection and knowledge generation. "At some point in a teacher's career, he/she must become a clinical supervisor of sorts because only the actors themselves can render the hermeneutic knowledge needed to understand teaching" (Garman 1990, p. 212). When teachers engage in the process of generating knowledge about their own teaching, they realize important benefits. "Their teaching is transformed in important ways: they become theorists articulating their intentions, testing their assumptions, and finding connections with practice" (Cochran-Smith and Lytle 1990, p. 8).

Supervisors as Collaborators in Creating Knowledge

Just as the teacher's role will change when students are seen as active partners in constructing knowledge, so too the supervisor's role will change when teachers are viewed as constructors of their own knowledge about learning and teaching. From its traditional perspective, supervision is viewed as a process intended to help teachers improve instruction. The supervisor often, intentionally or unintentionally, takes on the role of critic whose task is to judge the degree of congruence between the teacher's classroom behavior and the model of teaching that the teacher is trying to implement or the generic research on teaching.

When the supervisor is viewed as a critic who judges the teacher's performance, supervision tends to concentrate on surface-level issues because the supervisor is denied access by the teacher to the dilemmas, issues, and problems that every teacher experiences and struggles with on an ongoing basis (Blumberg and Jonas 1987). These dilemmas and problems reach to the very heart of the teaching enterprise and cannot be resolved by simply adding new models to our repertoires of teaching behaviors. They must be confronted head on and resolved through action and reflection in the classroom (Schön 1983). Supervision should play a central role in understanding and resolving complex, perennial problems such as:

- how to reconcile individual student needs and interests with group needs and interests;

- how to balance the need to preserve student self-esteem with the need to provide students with honest feedback on their performance;

- how to balance student motivation against the need to teach prescribed content that may not match students' current needs or interests; and

- how to maintain a reasonable amount of order while still allowing sufficient flexibility for the intellectual freedom needed to pursue complex topics and issues.

When the supervisor relinquishes the role of critic to assume the role of co-creator of knowledge about learning and teaching, the teacher is more willing to grant the supervisor access to these core issues and dilemmas of teaching because the teacher does not have to fear a critique from the supervisor. Relinquishing the role of critic also benefits the supervisor by removing the awesome burden of serving as judge, jury, and director of the supervisory process.

When supervision is viewed as a process for generating knowledge about learning and teaching, data collection is transformed from a mechanism for documenting behavior to a mechanism for collecting information. This information can be used to deepen both teacher's and supervisor's understanding of the consequences of resolving problems, dilemmas, and issues in alternative ways. Conferences are also transformed. In the traditional conference scenario, the supervisor provides a neat, well-documented list of praiseworthy behaviors as well as some suggestion for future improvement. When the supervisor relinquishes the role of critic, conferences become collaborative work sessions in which both teacher and supervisor try to make sense of the almost always messy data that are gathered in the process of relating teacher action to its consequences for learners. Finally, the outcomes of conferences are transformed. In most current practice, both partners sign written narrative critiques, which are filed away to collect dust until next year's observation. When teacher and supervisor become co-creators of knowledge, they produce jointly developed, tentative understandings of the learning-teaching process. These insights can then be tested against the reality of the classroom in future cycles of supervision.

To engage effectively in inquiry-oriented supervision, supervisors need a different type of expertise. They will need a passion for inquiry; commitment to developing an understanding of the process of learning and teaching; respect for teachers as equal partners in the process of trying to understand learning and teaching in the context of the teacher's particular classroom setting; and recognition that both partners contribute essential expertise to the process. They will also need to feel comfortable with the ambiguity and vulnerability of not having prefabricated answers to the problems that are encountered in the process. Supervisors will need to trust themselves, the teacher, and the process enough to believe that they can find reasonable and workable answers to complex questions and problems.

Greater Variety in Data Collection

The emphasis in traditional conceptions of learning on observable behavior, coupled with the emphasis on the teacher as the central actor, has resulted in the use of paper-and-pencil observation instruments as the primary and often sole vehicle for data gathering in supervision. When the supervisor's task is viewed as capturing the observable behavior of one actor (the teacher), paper-and-pencil instruments seem to work reasonably well. However, when learning is viewed as an active process of knowledge construction by the learner, student cognition becomes the critical element in the learning process. Learning is then seen as a collaborative process between teacher and learner, and the task of gathering useful data changes dramatically. Now, the data-gathering task becomes one of simultaneously capturing information about multiple actors which can be used to make inferences about the thinking processes that are occurring in the minds of the actors. This type of data collection requires supplementing paper-and-pencil instruments with a wide range of data-gathering techniques including audiotapes, videotapes, student products (essays, projects, tests), student interviews, and written student feedback regarding classroom events.

The use of multiple sources of data will bring about another important change in the expertise required of those who function as supervisors. The supervisor will need to become an expert in helping the teacher match various types of data collection strategies to the questions that are being addressed in the supervisory process and in helping the teacher interpret and reflect on the data that have been gathered. This change in the focus of data collection techniques will parallel closely the changes that have taken place in educational research techniques over the past decade. Just as the paper-and-pencil instruments used in the process-product research on teaching have been augmented by qualitative data collection strategies, so too observation and data collection in supervision can be expanded to include many more data sources. Data alone, however, are never sufficient. They never tell the full story. Only human judgment, in this case the collaborative judgment of teacher and supervisor, can give meaning to the richness of the learning-teaching process. Human judgment functions much more effectively in capturing that richness when it is augmented by a wide variety of data sources.

Garman (1990) points out an additional factor that comes into play when we view the goal of data collection as capturing student and teacher thinking: the development of thinking over time. Data collection currently is almost always accomplished by the observation of a single period of instruction.

> [A] lesson generally means an episodic event taken out of context within a larger unit of study. It is time to consider the unfolding lesson as a major concept in clinical supervision. We must find ways to capture how a teacher unfolds the content of a particular unit of study and how students, over time, encounter the content (Garman 1990, p. 212).

By collecting data over longer periods of instruction, we would be likely to obtain a much more complete picture of both teacher and student thinking. We would also capture a much richer portrait of the teacher's view of how the discipline should be represented for students. Although it might at first seem that collecting data over several periods of instruction requires additional time for observation by the supervisor, this is not necessarily the case. When the teacher becomes a collaborator in the process, and multiple data collection techniques are used (e.g., videotapes, student homework, student tests), the supervisor need not be present for every period of instruction during which data are gathered. The teacher can take primary responsibility for much of the data collection and then meet with the supervisor to jointly interpret and discuss the meaning of the data.

Greater Balance Between General Concerns and Content-Specific Issues and Questions

Given the renewed emphasis and research on content-specific learning and teaching, the focus of supervision should shift from total emphasis on general concerns to the inclusion of content-specific issues and questions. This does not mean that we should exclude general behaviors. To do so would clearly be a mistake because process-product research has been successful in identifying some behaviors that seem to transfer across content (Gage and Needels 1989). However, as Shulman (1987) has pointed out, excluding content-specific strategies from the supervisory process has also been a mistake. We need to balance content-specific issues and general issues.

On the surface at least, this need to expand the focus of supervision poses a dilemma for many schools. Principals, who supervise teachers in many different content areas, carry out much of the supervision that takes place in schools. The question is whether a generalist can be an effective supervisor when the supervisory process focuses not only on general concerns but also on content-specific strategies and methods. Given the new supervisory mindscape, we believe it is possible.

If the supervisor is viewed as a collaborator whose primary task is to help teachers reflect on and learn about their own teaching practices through the collection and interpretation of multiple sources of data, and the teacher who has content expertise is allowed to direct the process, it seems reasonable to think that content-specific issues could be addressed through supervision. In addition, if supervision is viewed as a function—not merely a role—to which many people in a school can contribute (Alfonso and Goldsberry 1982), it would also be possible to use a process of group supervision, peer coaching, or colleague consultation to help address content-specific issues, provided the peers have the appropriate preparation and skills.

Whatever personnel are used to carry out the process, the scope of supervision needs to be expanded to include questions such as these: What content should be taught to this group of students? Are the content and the instructional approaches being used compatible? What beliefs about the content and its general nature are being conveyed to students by the teacher's long-term approach to the subject matter? Are students acquiring the thinking and learning strategies that are most important for long-term success in the discipline?

Emphasis on Group Supervision

Just as students seem to benefit when they are placed in groups to cooperate with each other in the learning process, teachers seem to benefit when they are allowed to work together in groups to help each other learn about and refine the process of teaching (Little 1982). Teachers learn by watching each other teach. In addition, the new roles they take on and the perspectives they gain promote higher levels of thinking and cognitive development (Sprinthall and Thies-Sprinthall 1983). This benefits students because teachers who have reached higher cognitive-developmental levels tend to be more flexible and better able to meet individual student needs (Hunt and Joyce 1967). Collaborative practices have been endorsed and employed in staff development circles for several years; however, supervisory practice, which also aims at professional development, typically continues to occur on a one-to-one basis between supervisor and teacher.

We concur with Fullan (1990), who pointed out the necessity of linking collaboration to norms of continuous improvement:

> There is nothing particularly virtuous about collaboration per se. It can serve to block change or put students down as well as to elevate learning. Thus, collegiality must be linked to norms of continuous improvement and experimentation in which teachers are constantly seeking and assessing potentially better practices inside and outside their own school (p.15).

Similarly, group supervision must be viewed as an activity whose primary aim is learning about and improving teaching. Teachers are sometimes uncomfortable when they are asked to confront tough questions about their own teaching. Collaboration and mutual support from colleagues can be vehicles for enabling teachers to risk facing these tough questions. However, there is a danger that collaboration can be wrongly viewed as meaning to support one another without rocking the boat or causing any discomfort. When this happens, collaboration can degenerate into a mechanism for skirting tough questions through unwarranted assurances that things are just fine. To avoid this degeneration, all participants must understand that learning about the instructional process and improving student learning are the primary goals of group supervision. Collaboration is a means to an end, not an end in itself. It is a mechanism for providing support as teachers engage in the sometimes disquieting, uncomfortable process of learning.

Given the research on cooperative learning and teacher collegiality, we hypothesize that if supervision were carried out as a group process in which the supervisors and teachers were interdependent in achieving group and individual goals, the process of supervision would become more effective in helping teachers learn about and improve their teaching. In addition, enabling those teachers who may be less committed to growth to work together in groups with colleagues who are more committed to the process may be an effective strategy for creating shared norms that are supportive of the supervisory process. In discussing the concept of collaborative cultures, Hargreaves and Dawe (1989) eloquently describe what supervision might become when it is viewed as a cooperative group process. "It is a tool of teacher empowerment and professional enhancement, bringing colleagues and their expertise together to generate critical yet also practically-grounded reflection on what they do as a basis for more skilled action" (p. 7).

◆ ◆ ◆

What we have labeled "the changing mindscape on learning and teaching" demands a new mindscape on supervision, a mindscape grounded in the following principles and beliefs:

1. The primary purpose of supervision is to provide a mechanism for teachers and supervisors to increase their understanding of the learning-teaching process through collaborative inquiry with other professionals.

2. Teachers should not be viewed only as consumers of research, but as generators of knowledge about learning and teaching.

3. Supervisors must see themselves not as critics of teaching performance, but rather as collaborators with teachers in attempting to understand the problems, issues, and dilemmas that are inherent in the process of learning and teaching.

4. Acquiring an understanding of the learning-teaching process demands the collection of many types of data, over extended periods of time.

5. The focus for supervision needs to be expanded to include content-specific as well as general issues and questions.

6. Supervision should focus not only on individual teachers but also on groups of teachers who are engaged in ongoing inquiry concerning common problems, issues, and questions.

These principles and beliefs are not completely new. They closely parallel the principles of clinical supervision as endorsed by Cogan (1973) and Goldhammer (1969). Unfortunately, these principles have not been widely adopted. We believe that the changing perspectives on learning and teaching provide a powerful impetus for putting these principles of supervision into practice. When these concepts begin to touch the mainstream of supervisory practice, supervision is much more likely to have a positive impact on teacher thinking, teacher behavior, and student learning.

References

Alfonso, R.J., and L. Goldsberry. (1982). "Colleagueship in Supervision." In *Supervision of Teaching,* edited by T.J. Sergiovanni. Alexandria, Va.: ASCD.

Anderson, L.M. (1989). "Classroom Instruction." In *Knowledge Base for the Beginning Teacher,* edited by M.C. Reynolds. New York: Pergamon Press and the American Association of Colleges of Teacher Education.

Blumberg, A., and R.D. Jonas. (1987). "Permitting Access: The Teacher's Control Over Supervision." *Educational Leadership* 44, 8: 12–16.

Brandt, R. (1988–89). "On Learning Research: A Conversation with Lauren Resnick." *Educational Leadership* 46, 4: 12–16.

Brandt, R. (1989–90). "On Cooperative Learning: A Conversation with Spencer Kagan." *Educational Leadership* 47, 4: 8–11.

Bransford, J.D., and N.J. Vye. (1989). "A Perspective on Cognitive Research and Its Implications for Instruction." In *Toward the Thinking Curriculum: Current Cognitive Research,* edited by L.B. Resnick and L.E. Klopfer. Alexandria, Va.: ASCD.

Brooks, J.G. (1990). "Teachers and Students: Constructivists Forging New Connections." *Educational Leadership* 47, 5: 68–71.

Buchman, M. (1984). "The Priority of Knowledge and Understanding in Teaching." In *Advances in Teacher Education* Vol. 1, edited by L.G. Katz and J.D. Raths. Norwood, N.J.: Ablex.

Cochran-Smith, M., and S.L. Lytle. (1990). "Research on Teaching and Teacher Research: Issues That Divide." *Educational Researcher* 19, 2: 2–11.

Cogan, M. (1973). *Clinical Supervision.* Boston: Houghton-Mifflin.

Dewey, J. (1902). *The Child and the Curriculum.* Chicago: University of Chicago Press.

Fullan, M. (1990). "Staff Development, Innovation, and Institutional Development." In *Changing School Culture Through Staff Development. The 1990 ASCD Yearbook,* edited by B. Joyce. Alexandria, Va.: ASCD.

Gage, N.L., and M.C. Needels. (1989). "Process-Product Research on Teaching: A Review of Criticisms." *Elementary School Journal* 89, 3: 253–300.

Garman, N.B. (1986). "Reflection: The Heart of Clinical Supervision: A Modern Rationale for Professional Practice." *Journal of Curriculum and Supervision* 2, 1:1–24.

Garman, N.B. (1990). "Theories Embedded in the Events of Clinical Supervision: A Hermeneutic Approach." *Journal of Curriculum and Supervision* 5, 3: 201–213.

Goldhammer, R. (1969). *Clinical Supervision: Special Methods for the Supervision of Teachers.* New York: Holt, Rinehart, and Winston.

Hargreaves, A., and R. Dawe. (1989). "Coaching as Unreflective Practice." Paper presented at the Annual Meeting of the American Educational Research Association, San Francisco.

Henry, G. (1986). "What Is the Nature of English Education?" *English Education* 18, 1: 4–41.

Hunt, D.E., and B.R. Joyce. (1967). "Teacher Trainee Personality and Initial Teaching Style." *American Educational Research Journal* 4: 253–59.

Joyce, B., and B. Showers. (1988). *Student Achievement Through Staff Development.* New York: Longman.

Lampert, M. (1990). "When the Problem Is Not the Question and the Solution Is Not the Answer: Mathematical Knowing and Teaching." *American Educational Research Journal* 27, 1: 29–63.

Little, J. (1982). "Norms of Collegiality and Experimentation: Workplace Conditions of School Success." *American Educational Research Journal* 5, 19: 325–340.

Perkins, D.N., and G. Salomon. (1989). "Are Cognitive Skills Context-Bound?" *Educational Researcher* 8, 1: 16–25.

Putnam, R. (1990). "Recipes and Reflective Learning: 'What Would Prevent You from Saying It That Way?'" Paper presented at the Annual Meeting of the American Educational Research Association, Boston.

Resnick, L.B., and L.E. Klopfer. (1989). *Toward the Thinking Curriculum: Current Cognitive Research.* Alexandria, Va: ASCD.

Schlechty, P.C. (1990). *Schools for the 21st Century.* San Francisco: Jossey-Bass.

Schön, D.A. (1983). *The Reflective Practitioner.* San Francisco: Jossey-Bass.

Schön, D.A. (1989). "Coaching Reflective Teaching." In *Reflection in Teacher Education,* edited by P.P. Grimmet and G.P. Erickson. New York: Teachers College Press.

Sergiovanni, T.J. (1985). "Landscapes, Mindscapes, and Reflective Practice in Supervision." *Journal of Curriculum and Supervision* 1, 1: 5–17.

Shulman, L.S. (1987). "Knowledge and Teaching: Foundations of the New Reform." *Harvard Educational Review* 57: 1–22.

Shulman, L.S. (1990). "Transformation of Content Knowledge." Paper presented at the Annual Meeting of the American Educational Research Association, Boston.

Slavin, R.E. (1989–90). "Research on Cooperative Learning: Consensus and Controversy." *Educational Leadership* 47, 4: 52–54.

Sprinthall, N.A., and L. Thies-Sprinthall. (1983). "The Teacher as Adult Learner: A Cognitive Developmental View." In *Staff Development. 82nd Yearbook of the National Society for the Study of Education,* edited by G.A. Griffin. Chicago: University of Chicago Press.

Wilson, S.M., L.S. Shulman, and A.E. Richert. (1987). "150 Different Ways of Knowing: Representations of Knowledge in Teaching." In *Exploring Teachers' Thinking,* edited by J. Calderhead. London: Cassel.

1

A Teacher Who Is Working to Change Her Practice

The article in this section, assigned as homework reading before the second session of *Lenses on Learning, Module 3,* serves as a backdrop for the focus on classroom observation and teacher supervision in this module.

READING 2 "What's So Special About Math? Lisa Yaffee" (Schifter and Fosnot)

This reading is a chapter from a longer book of case studies that offers a valuable look at both the practical and emotional sides of teachers who are "meeting the challenge of reform" in mathematics education. Some administrators may feel especially empathetic with the subject of this chapter, Lisa Yaffee—a math-phobic teacher working hard to increase her own mathematical knowledge while simultaneously working to change her mathematics teaching practice.

Take notes or use highlighters as you read. Think about and be prepared to discuss the following questions:

- What did Ms. Yaffee know to begin with, and what did she have to learn?

- What were some of the central elements of Ms. Yaffee's struggle?

- What was Ms. Yaffee's mathematical agenda for her students? What was her mathematical agenda for herself? How were they connected?

What's So Special About Math? Lisa Yaffee

Deborah Schifter and Catherine Twomey Fosnot

Participating in SummerMath for Teachers has changed almost every aspect of the classroom curriculum—not just math!

> Donna Natowich
> Green Street School
> Brattleboro, VT

Several years ago I became involved in Whole Language and Process Writing and worked very hard to change the way I taught language arts. When I did that, I found that it changed the way I taught almost everything—everything except math.

> Nancy Lawrence
> Wolf Swamp Road School
> Longmeadow, MA

As their mathematics instruction begins to reflect the influence of constructivist principles, many teachers report that their practice in other disciplinary areas has been affected as well. "It has altered the way I think about teaching." "I ask different kinds of questions now." "I'm really listening to my students." "It has even changed the way I deal with discipline!"

Significantly, however, teachers who develop a constructivist-oriented classroom practice in writing, say, or social studies, or the sciences, typically find their approach to mathematics unaffected by analogous innovations. This is often true despite the acute dissatisfaction they may come to feel with their mathematics work. . . .

AUTHOR NOTE: Lisa Yaffee participated in a professional development program called SummerMath for Teachers, which started with a summer institute and included classroom follow-up. Six months into the program, she also enrolled in a mathematics course for elementary teachers, taught by SummerMath for Teachers staff. The institute, the follow-up program, and the mathematics course are described in *Reconstructing Mathematics Education,* the book from which this chapter is taken.

The inability of teachers to translate alternative pedagogical approaches into their mathematics instruction likely stems from several related causes: first, they share the generally prevalent conception of mathematics, in which inquiry, exploration, and vigorous debate play little or no role; second, those charged with teaching mathematics do not themselves understand the material well enough even to conceive of an alternative practice; and third, most teachers do not have enough confidence in themselves as mathematical thinkers to allow themselves to contemplate a shift toward teaching for a qualitatively different kind of understanding. Additional discouragement may come because students' habits and preconceptions—formed in the culture of the traditional mathematics classroom and reflecting again the larger society's attitude toward mathematics—are often highly resistant to the changes such a shift implies.

Lisa Yaffee, the subject of this chapter, is not typical of the teachers who enroll in SummerMath for Teachers. After college she spent a year in El Paso, Texas, as a VISTA volunteer, later wrote for a feminist newsletter at MIT, where she worked as a secretary, and later still worked with emotionally disturbed and learning-disabled students aged 8 to 22. She attended Bank Street College for her pre-service education and at age 35, when she entered the program, had been teaching for only a year. Lisa is more outspoken than most, more articulate than most, and willing to challenge others as well as herself.

Yet, though she is not typical, and precisely because she is articulate and outspoken, her story shows what can happen to a teacher with a strong appreciation of constructivism and a real commitment to independent thinking when she changes her ideas about mathematics, and as her confidence in her ability to understand it grows.

Lisa's Background

Even before entering SummerMath for Teachers, Lisa envisioned a classroom in which students' active involvement was both the goal and the instrument of learning. Her very reason for becoming a teacher was to help her students develop strong voices. "I came to teaching as a form of social action," she explained, "one which would be more enabling for kids than organizing their parents politically." Thus, her conception of classroom process was already a sharp departure from the traditional classroom in which the teacher tells her students what they should know. "I had an image of [the] teacher as street-fighter, [social activist], not as answerman."

At Bank Street, Lisa received a foundation in pedagogical theory that she described as "developmental/constructivist/Piagetian." She had chosen Bank Street because of its emphasis on pre-service classroom experience. She was surprised to find that "most [courses] were good!"—the exception was an acutely disappointing mathematics methods course. "[It] was the least satisfying . . . course I took. . . . Although there was plenty of 'hands-on'. . . there wasn't enough minds-on for my taste."

Once Lisa began teaching, she was happy with her programs in language arts, science, and social studies, but was concerned that her mathematics instruction was not meeting her fifth and sixth graders' needs. "I didn't teach any math," Lisa later explained:

I'm embarrassed to admit this but it's true. . . . I just sort of handed the kids a math book. I gave them a placement test at the beginning of the year. I let them work at their own pace and it was pretty individualized and that's how math is being taught in most of this building, from what I could observe. I knew it wasn't working. I felt awful about that. . . . But I didn't know what else to do. I really felt strongly that I didn't know how to teach math.

Lisa was quite aware, however, that her problems had not begun at Bank Street . . . [and] she looked back to the very beginnings of her formal schooling to locate the source of her difficulties. As far back as she could remember, she had been an unsuccessful mathematics student, having learned how to "get by," even as she understood that she was missing the essence.

Learning [math] from first grade on always followed a pattern: observe teacher or kids, record in the memory or on paper, see what others have recorded, respond. I experienced a certain amount of disequilibrium as I learned how to please, but mostly I assimilated and accommodated . . . everything and everyone. . . . Math was a language I couldn't master. I knew the vocabulary but didn't understand what it meant or how to apply it. I did my best to fake the pattern here.

It was generally believed—by teachers, by family, by Lisa herself—that she was among those people who "do not have a math mind."

I allowed myself to accept what the "objective" results of tests and teacher response to my muddled efforts at math suggested, namely that I couldn't understand it and never would. . . . As an artist, [loosely] defined . . . , I was missing out on a thrilling set of descriptors.

Getting Started

During her first year of teaching, Lisa attended a series of four afternoon workshops conducted by former SummerMath for Teachers participants where she had no trouble recognizing an approach to mathematics instruction consistent with her beliefs about what education should be. She saw that mathematics could be taught through problem solving using manipulatives, so for the rest of that year she included problem-solving sessions in her mathematics instruction. But Lisa was acutely aware that she did not know how to integrate this work with her charge of teaching arithmetic, geometry, and other mathematics content. Thus, in her program application, she presented a fairly well-defined statement of what she wanted to learn:

1. How do you organize your math program around problem solving?

2. How do you introduce new concepts?

3. How do you structure problems so that previous knowledge of algorithms doesn't block hands-on thinking?

4. How do you teach abstract concepts like exponents and division of fractions with manipulatives?

She also saw that in order to teach effectively, she, too, needed to learn mathematics.

I'm hoping to gain a greater conceptual understanding of math processes, of math as a language and of the fearful symmetry underlying the whole mess. I hope to acquire some confidence in [my] ability to think my way out of a mathematical bag, as it were, so I can encourage and nurture that kind of confidence for my kids. . . . I'd like to feel convinced that exponents *do* relate to me personally (beyond the third dimension). In addition to getting some answers to my questions, I'm looking forward to developing the capacity to ask new ones. Please let me come!

Lisa did attend the institute, but exposure to new possibilities aroused conflicting feelings. On the one hand, she knew that she wanted to change and she saw that SummerMath for Teachers offered an approach consistent with her beliefs. On the other, as much as Lisa was poised to develop a new mathematics teaching practice, her glimpse of the big picture frightened her. Primed to react to a cascade of new insights but not quite knowing how to do so, she raged, furious at the institute and the staff:

What the institute has done is to take away our sense of control. We're supposed to live in the dorm. If we don't, we're missing something. We have our meals and classes at designated times. We do things we hate. We're bombarded with alien stimuli until we're exhausted. These experiences do not compute and we get no processing time. In short, we've been thrown into chaos. . . .

I could go on and on. Instead I'll summarize. This week I learned what it feels like to be a pre-operational [or] concrete-operational kid contending with formal-operational expectations. It's hard, frustrating, overwhelming, infuriating, demeaning, terrifying and depressing.

Yet, despite her rage, Lisa was developing a sense of how constructivist theory might apply to mathematics instruction. In her synthesis paper she argued that:

You can teach kids how to manipulate material without "teaching" them understanding. It means that you can't "teach" understanding because the way each person understands is arrived at uniquely. . . . It also means that the teacher has to set up conditions under which every student arrives. Somehow the kids have to be able to structure a problem or concept so they can understand it. Your construct probably won't help.

However, the development of a pedagogical vision, or the refinement of one, was not what Lisa felt she needed at the time. She wanted specific answers to specific questions and at the end of the institute she felt no better equipped to act on new understandings of how mathematics is learned than she had when the session began. In a paper discussing the implications for the classroom of her current theory of learning, she wrote:

I can answer superficially and cosmetically, according to what teaching should look like, but I don't know how to achieve the effect. I'm not sure how to set up an environment in which kids really learn math, as opposed to one in which they learn how to manipulate materials. It is frustrating to be this stupid, to leave the institute bearing the same burden of needs I carried in with me. I still don't know how to build a math curriculum around hands-on problem solving or how to think mathematically (whatever that is). I still don't understand how to use manipulatives to teach abstract concepts like fractions. On top of the old agenda is grafted a new one: how to help kids refine cumbersome or confusing notation systems which might impede learning, how to probe so that students refine or discard ill-conceived theories in which magic or ignorance account for what's happening mathematically; and lastly, how to show the connection between what students "know," or *really* understand, and what they're supposed to know, namely the abstract operations with algorithms on which they'll be tested and by which results their positions in society will ultimately (and criminally) be determined.

Despite her rage, Lisa had found the important questions. She was frightened by her new knowledge and angry at the implied expectation that it was up to her to figure out how to "do it." But now she needed to find the breathing space and the confidence to begin to construct answers—in her own classroom and with her own students.

With some trepidation, Deborah visited Lisa's classroom for the first time in mid-September following the institute. [Deborah, who had directed the summer institute, provided follow-up by visiting Lisa in her classroom on a weekly basis.] Arriving early, she observed the last 10 minutes of Lisa's social studies class and saw how respectfully Lisa listened and responded to her students' opinions on current events. This aspect of classroom instruction came very naturally to her and was not new.

Then, as math class began, Lisa brought out a set of base-ten blocks she had found abandoned deep in the school's storage closet. "We'll be working with just the special-needs kids today," she told Deborah. "I think I'm going to teach multiplication, but I don't know how."

But before Lisa had had an opportunity to introduce the lesson, her students, who had never used the blocks before, began to build towers with them. Lisa looked at Deborah, smiled, and shrugged. Her students were determined not to let anything interfere until their towers were built, so the adults just sat back and watched. When Melinda was satisfied her tower was finished, Lisa asked her how much, in terms of the values of the blocks, it was worth. As the other students finished with theirs, they came around to check out Melinda's, suggesting their own counting schemes. The rest of the lesson involved sharing counting schemes for all the towers the students had built.

"I had to go with where they were," Lisa explained in her conference with Deborah after class. "I saw they had to become familiar with the materials. But what mathematics did they do?"

Deborah proposed they analyze the various counting strategies, and then they discussed how these schemes illustrated properties of the number system—commutativity and distributivity—as well as providing practice in addition and multiplication of four-digit numbers. By the end of the conversation, Lisa realized that she and her students had been engaged in mathematics after all, and she had a few ideas about how to continue the following day.

Within just a few weeks of that initial visit and discussion, Lisa began to feel growing confidence and excitement. She was thirsty to learn, and able to articulate what she was learning. After a workshop for participating elementary teachers early in October, she described her changing conception of the nature of mathematics:

> For me the real revelation today was to discover that math is really like every other subject. I never realized that math is learning how to ask questions and how to think about the questions you ask. I knew this about literature, political science, biology, etc. Why it never occurred to me about math eludes me.

She then reflected parenthetically on just why mathematics had occupied its own special category for her: "Too much trauma associated with math and learning math? Maybe traumas of the past explain why I flipped out this summer!"

Learning Mathematics

This change in Lisa's conception of mathematics allowed her to look at her curriculum in a new way. As she and her students reviewed whole-number operations that fall, she became intrigued by the patterns and relationships she began to see, and shared both her excitement and her questions with her students. Soon they, too, were finding patterns and exploring why they worked.

Though she was pleased with the changes that were taking place in her mathematics class, Lisa was aware that they were not enough. "I don't know enough math to teach effectively," she explained. "It is imperative to keep learning more math to be able to teach it well."

Lisa took on her commitment to learn mathematics with great seriousness. Each week she prepared for Deborah's visit by compiling a list of questions, both pedagogical and mathematical. In response to her interest, Deborah brought problems for her to work on at home. At the end of January, Lisa began a mathematics course for elementary teachers taught by Deborah.

Aware of the centrality of fractions in the fifth- and sixth-grade curriculum and of the difficulties children have with them, Lisa decided to make fractions the focus of her study that year. Specifically, she set as her goal understanding the contexts in which multiplication and/or division of fractions is called for. Lisa's journal account of her own process of working on decimal problems (taken from Harel et al., 1989, and Owens, 1988) illustrates her tenacity, as well as the rigorous expectations she had for herself:

> *1. On a highway, a four-wheel-drive car can go 7.5 km on each liter of gasoline. How many kilometers can the car be expected to go on 1.3 liters?*

> $1.3 \times 7.5 = 9.75$ km. At first I was going to divide, but then realized that in order to find 1.3 of something you need to multiply. I don't really understand why this is true and didn't (don't) understand why certain problems imply multiplication with fractions either. The only confidence I have that this answer is probably right comes from knowing that the car can go further on 1.3 liters than on 1 liter, so the answer has to be greater than 7.5 by $\frac{3}{10}$ [of 7.5].

2. Tom spent $900.00 for 0.75 kg of platinum. What would be the price of 1 kg bar of platinum?

The way I did this one was to convert to fractions. $\frac{3}{4}$ of x = 900 so $\frac{1}{4}$ [of x] = 300. Add 300 to 900 and you get 1,200. 1 kg would cost $\frac{1}{4}$ more and you already know what $\frac{3}{4}$ [is]. I wouldn't know by just looking at the decimal problem which operation to use without first going through what I just described.

While she solved each problem successfully, Lisa was still dissatisfied. She was looking for the generalizations that characterize multiplication and division, but as yet they eluded her.

On the decimal homework I had more trouble than I thought I would and my problems are the same as the ones I have with fractions. I couldn't see immediately . . . what operation to use for problem 1 and had to think it through as a fraction problem. I found myself doing that a couple of times, in fact, and always on the problems where the operation of choice is multiplication. This shows me the conceptual connections between decimals and fractions and also that I still don't understand what multiplication is. This really bugs me.

Over the next week, Lisa continued to struggle with the same issues:

1. Each package of typing paper weighs 0.55 kg. Adam used 0.35 of a package for his research paper. How many kilograms of paper did he use?

.55 × .35 = .1925—multiply. You want to know what a little more than $\frac{1}{3}$ of $\frac{1}{2}$ is. For formulistic reasons that I'll probably never understand, to find a fraction of something, multiply. The answer should be a little more than $\frac{1}{6}$. .1925 is almost $\frac{1}{5}$ so that makes sense to me.

2. Marissa bought 0.46 of a pound of wheat flour for which she paid $0.83. How many pounds of flour could she buy for $1.00?

I can't really do anything with this problem. It's kind of abstract. Marissa paid almost a dollar to get almost $\frac{1}{2}$ lb of flour, so if she paid a whole dollar she would probably get close to a $\frac{1}{2}$ lb or a little more. Instinct says divide something into something else so you can get a price-per-pound figure, but I don't immediately see what. The voice of memory says .46/.83 as x/1.00.

.83x = .46

x = .5542168, which according to my initial, "common-sense" reasonings is a plausible answer.

Again, even though Lisa was able to solve each problem correctly, she was after a deeper level of understanding. What is it in the structure of each of the problems that determines which operation to use?

"More Decimals" brought up more of the same previous issues: namely, that I don't understand multiplication and division of fractions or decimals. Problem 1 was easy. On problem 2, I began by thinking that I couldn't solve it because I couldn't get my mind around it. I knew it was a division problem but couldn't explain why and therefore couldn't tell what to divide into what. Then I went to simple algebra, because I knew I could solve the problem that way, from memory. Whenever I go to algebra it is a cop-out. It means that I can't derive what the problem is about at its core or what to do about it just based on "logic" and the information given. I had this same series of traumas with all these problems, as I explained in the homework protocols.

What interests me about this is how dissatisfied I feel . . . when I can't derive an answer "logically." I don't care how valuable math instinct (unconscious) is, it doesn't help me feel that I understand, in any kind of profound way, what's going on in a math problem. Knowing what to do isn't any good. I need to know why.

Lisa was doing more than simply solving problems. She was searching for patterns that would allow her to construct the general principles that govern the operations. She knew that understanding had to come from within. She could listen endlessly to other people's explanations and read innumerable articles about fractions, but she had to construct the ideas. Without that, all of the rest was mere empty verbiage:

I am still struggling with multiplication of fractions. Why is $\frac{1}{4}$ of 40 a multiplication problem? From the Driscoll article [1983] I got a new label for this idea—fraction as "operator," but I don't know what this means.

As her instructor, Deborah wondered why Lisa was so unhappy with herself when she was clearly doing so much good mathematical thinking. She could solve all the problems and verify each solution with sound reasoning. Was her self-condemnation the result of habit? All her life Lisa had thought of herself as a failure in mathematics. Was she unable to give up that aspect of her identity?

By the end of the course, it became clear that this was not the explanation. Lisa was looking for a kind of mathematical thinking in herself that she could recognize and respect once she thought she had achieved it.

For example, an activity sheet on area and perimeter included a problem that required drawing a trapezoid whose area was 36 square units. Lisa worked on this problem by drawing a series of trapezoids, each with an altitude of 4 units. Her first guess had bases of 15 and 7 units; her second had bases of 14 and 6 units; and her third had bases of 13 and 5 units. (See Figure 1.) Not only had she solved the problem from the activity sheet, she had also discovered a pattern: "Every time you eliminate one unit from the bases, you lose four square units of area if the altitude is 4."

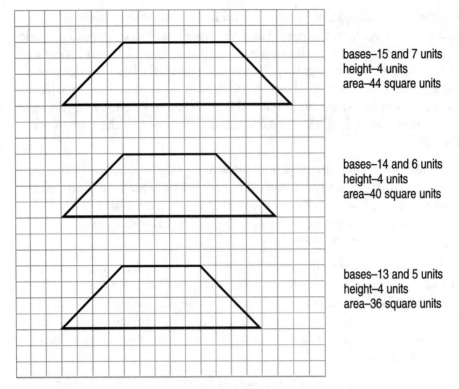

bases–15 and 7 units
height–4 units
area–44 square units

bases–14 and 6 units
height–4 units
area–40 square units

bases–13 and 5 units
height–4 units
area–36 square units

Figure 1. Searching for a trapezoid whose area is 36 square units

Curious about this discovery, Lisa now wanted to check trapezoids with other altitudes. When she drew one with bases 7 and 1, altitude 3, and another with bases 8 and 2, altitude 3, she saw that the area of the second had increased by 3 square units. (See Figure 2.) She described her process in her journal:

> I got into problem 15 and fooled around with trapezoids for a while. I noticed a pattern which was a little more complicated than the things I generally notice. I was also able to verbalize it more clearly and precisely than usual. Then I actually had enough curiosity (excitement? investment?) in this discovery to try to generalize from it, which may be a first for me. I also had a dim sense or suspicion of what it might be all about. I patted myself on the figurative back and said, Hey, you're improving. Your thinking is becoming a little more sophisticated, more precise. You're finding ways to test ideas. (You're actually *having* math ideas.) I had been working a pretty long time. I was perfectly satisfied with what I had "accomplished" because it was more than I expected to.

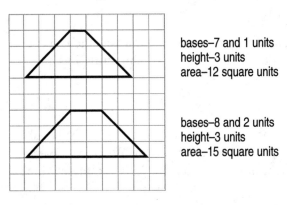

bases–7 and 1 units
height–3 units
area–12 square units

bases–8 and 2 units
height–3 units
area–15 square units

Figure 2. Testing a conjecture: if the altitude is n units, increasing the bases by one unit will increase the area by n square units

Lisa then described how she had gone for a walk and, when she returned, had sat down to continue her journal entry. And as she did so, she suddenly realized she could draw a diagram to explain the pattern she had discovered. (See Lisa's diagram in Figure 3.)

> I all of a sudden could explain the pattern I saw, and I'm pretty sure I'm right.

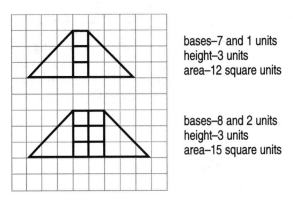

bases–7 and 1 units
height–3 units
area–12 square units

bases–8 and 2 units
height–3 units
area–15 square units

Figure 3. Lisa's demonstration convinced her of the truth of her conjecture

> This whole process just described illustrates what it means to know a minuscule portion of mathematics, but it is certainly a starting point and I'm thrilled. Previous to this I would describe what I had learned since SummerMath as knowledge *about* mathematics, but I think that finally I'm beginning to know math and to understand, in a way that's meaningful to me personally, what that knowledge is. Feels good.

Now, after one year, Lisa was able to recognize that she had met the goal she had set for herself in her summer institute application: to acquire some confidence in her ability to think mathematically. Early in the year she had seen mathematics as a search for patterns and an exploration of the relationships among them. As she began to discover patterns she wished to explore, she could now generalize and show why those patterns must hold.

Teaching Mathematics

As Lisa worked on her own mathematical understanding, what was the impact on her teaching? Let us go back to December to see what was happening in her classroom.

Episodes from a unit on fractions

Near the end of her unit on whole numbers, Lisa confessed to Deborah that she was scared of starting fractions. "I don't know where to begin. We don't have any manipulatives, so I can't just hand them out and watch the kids. Besides, I don't even understand fractions myself!"

In response, Deborah gave Lisa a bare outline of where to start and what to cover—what fractions are, equivalent fractions, and operations—and handed her a set of nonroutine fraction problems to explore on her own. While working on these, Lisa accepted the challenge of devising her own problem sets for her students. To that end, she had to analyze fraction operations and think up physical situations that modeled them.

One day in early December, Deborah entered Lisa's school and, heading for her classroom, found several students sprawled in the hallways outside her door. As Deborah entered the room, she saw the rest of the class either lying on the floor or bent over the table, working on large sheets of oak tag.

"Hi," said Lisa. "We got started early today. They're making their fraction bars."

Deborah squatted down to watch Sonia, who had divided her sheet of oak tag into horizontal strips, each three inches wide. The top one was labeled "one whole"; the second was divided into two equal parts, each labeled "$\frac{1}{2}$"; the third was divided into three equal parts, and so on. Sonia was now working on the seventh strip.

"Shoot," she said. "It's still not coming out evenly."

Indeed, Deborah saw that Sonia had marked off six equal segments, but that the last one on the end was much larger than the others.

"We didn't have commercially made manipulatives for fractions," Lisa was to explain later,

> so we made fraction bars because [the students] needed some kind of physical representation. They'd measure it out and decide what one third was, one half, fourths, fifths, sixths. So by the time we got to doing problems, they knew all about equivalent fractions and all about like denominators—from creating them.

> There was a lot of discussion. You had an 18-inch whole; how do you divide that into sevenths? It won't go in evenly. And so it took them a while to figure out that you take that piece at the end and divide that into sevenths, and if you still have a little piece at the end you divide that into sevenths and then you have to figure out how to add those pieces to make each individual [seventh of the 18 inches]. It took them a while to figure out how to do it. It was very interesting.

Lisa understood that the purpose of making the fraction bars was not just to have them to use later, that making them was a valuable learning exercise in itself. She committed a full two weeks to the process to make sure the students learned how to use a ruler, understood that the pieces in each strip must be equal, and fully addressed any other questions that arose—how to make sevenths, for example.

> Then we cut all the pieces out [and laminated them] and put them in some kind of order. We talked about what the order was and what the rule was. Some kids put them all in wholes and some kids went from tiniest to bigger and some kids went with pieces that would fit evenly in other pieces [for example, halves, fourths, eighths; then thirds, sixths, twelfths, etc.]. So all of them were different.

By listening to her students as they worked at these activities, Lisa had the opportunity to find out what they understood so that she could plan the next phase of study. As she structured each activity of the unit, she considered what her students knew, what they didn't yet understand, and what they needed eventually to learn.

> The first problem set was pretty easy. I made the problems the weekend before I'd use them. . . . I'd watched [the students] with the fraction bars and I knew how much they knew already, so I didn't have to do anything with $\frac{1}{2} + \frac{1}{2}$. I could do really hard stuff—multiple-step problems. I knew that from watching them and interacting with them. I listened to their arguments about what patterns existed.

On a later visit, Deborah found Lisa's students working from another of her problem sets. Some of the students had gathered in pairs, some in groups of three or four; some worked alone first and then joined others to discuss the problems. Deborah sat down on the floor next to André, who had a pile of fraction pieces next to him.

"See, the problems are all about what kids in the class did over vacation," André told her. "This one's about Kwan Minh. *Kwan Minh and her family went skiing for December vacation. They spent $\frac{3}{5}$ of their time on the slopes and $\frac{2}{6}$ of their time riding to the top of the mountain. What fraction of their time was spent in the lodge sipping hot chocolate?*"

Knowing that Deborah would ask him what he was doing to solve the problem, André started explaining even before she had a chance to ask. "So this is what I have to do. This whole strip stands for the whole time of the ski trip. Then I've got $\frac{2}{6}$ and $\frac{3}{5}$." André sifted through his fraction pieces, selected the appropriate ones, and lined them up on top of the whole strip. "I've got to figure out what fits into that last section. The $\frac{1}{9}$ is too big," he said, testing it out. "So is the $\frac{1}{10}$, and so is the $\frac{1}{12}$. The $\frac{1}{15}$ looks pretty good."

Deborah looked down and saw that the $\frac{1}{15}$ did look pretty good. But André's fraction pieces hadn't been measured and cut accurately. Everything was just a bit off, and that $\frac{1}{15}$ hung over the edge of the strip underneath just a little.

But again, André was ahead of Deborah's questions. "It's just a little bit off," he said, "so now I have to figure out if it's because my pieces are a little off or if it's really not exactly $\frac{1}{15}$."

André wrote down: $\frac{2}{6} + \frac{3}{5} + ? = 1$.

"So," he explained. "I can't add them like that. I have to change the numbers. See, I can make the $\frac{2}{6}$ into $\frac{4}{12}$, but that doesn't help, and $\frac{8}{24}$ doesn't help either. Oh, wait! $\frac{2}{6}$ is the same as $\frac{1}{3}$. So, let's see, $\frac{1}{9}$s? $\frac{1}{12}$s? $\frac{1}{15}$s? ? Yeah! I can use $\frac{1}{15}$s—$\frac{2}{6}$ is the same as $\frac{1}{3}$, and that's the same as $\frac{5}{15}$. And $\frac{3}{5}$ is the same as $\frac{9}{15}$." And he wrote down on his paper: $\frac{5}{15} + \frac{9}{15} + ? = 1$.

"See, look. This comes out to $\frac{14}{15}$," he said, pointing to $\frac{5}{15} + \frac{9}{15}$. "So this has to be $\frac{1}{15}$. I was right; it's $\frac{1}{15}$."

What might have been a liability of these homemade manipulatives had, in this case, actually become an asset. Having made the fraction bars himself, André was fully aware of their inaccuracy. While they provided a representation that allowed him to picture the terms of the problem, they did not give him an answer. He knew that "close enough" was not satisfactory, and the inaccuracy of the manipulatives forced him to think through the mathematical structures in order to conclude finally that, yes, Kwan Minh had spent $\frac{1}{15}$ of her skiing vacation sipping hot chocolate.

Lisa described the classroom interactions that had preceded André's solution to the problem:

> At the beginning [the problems] all had like denominators, addition and subtraction. Toward the end of that problem set I threw in a couple of easy unlike denominators. Then we tried to derive what the rules were for addition of fractions for like denominators and addition of fractions for unlike denominators. I realized they couldn't really verbalize what the rules were for addition of fractions for unlike denominators, so we needed some more problems.

In each problem set, Lisa always included a few problems that addressed the next topic to be covered. In this way she would assess what her students already understood and where their difficulties lay.

> What I do the next day is based on what I observe and what I hear, how well the kids are able to verbalize what they're doing, how interested they seem. . . . What I'd do is always throw these teasers in and then they'd realize they needed more information and of course I wouldn't tell them. So then I'd be compelled to design more problems. . . .

> [In response to the teasers, they'd say,] I can't do this! And I'd go, Well, why can't you? Well, because you can't add those things. Well, show me with the fraction bars. They'd say, Well, it's easy, you just do this and this. And I'd say, Write an equation that shows what you just did. And that's the hard part. And I really pushed that.

Some weeks later, the class was working on multiplication. They were all sitting in a semicircle, some in chairs and some on the floor, looking at the blackboard. "How can that be?" asked Ivan. "You just said that was a half. Now you're saying it's a fourth."

Larry was up at the board pointing to his diagram. "Look, the problem says Lelieta's sister left her half the cake. So, see, here's the whole cake and here's the half that her sister left. Now, Lelieta didn't eat that whole half. She ate only half of it." Larry was marking off the amount Lelieta had eaten, pressing the chalk down as hard as he could. "So, it's a fourth of the cake. See? It's a half of what her sister left, but it's a fourth of the cake."

"What do you think, Ivan?" Lisa asked.

"Yeah, I guess. It's like, if I watch half an hour of TV, that doesn't mean that I watched half the night. Just because it's half an hour doesn't mean it's half of everything."

"Can anybody paraphrase what Ivan and Larry are saying?"

The discussion continued, going through other problems the students had worked on, examining how a given amount might be represented by different fractions. By the end of the period, Lisa felt that her students' understanding of that idea was solid enough for the class to be given another question to wrestle with.

"You know, we said earlier that all these problems were multiplication problems. And you all know how to solve them. Well, here's something else to think about. When we worked on multiplication with whole numbers, we understood it to be repeated addition. Right?"

All the students looked at her and nodded.

"But look at this. $\frac{1}{2} \times \frac{1}{4} = \frac{1}{8}$. I can't see any way in which anything is repeated. So if it's no longer repeated addition, what is multiplication?"

On that note, the math period ended and the students went off to music class.

When Deborah returned a week later, Lisa told her what had happened the following day. "Remember the question I posed? Well, the next day I asked it again at the beginning of the period, and we talked about it for a long time. By the end of the class, everyone was completely confused. So then they turned to me and said, 'Well, what's the answer?' And I said, 'I don't know. I'm as confused as you are.' So then they got really mad and said I shouldn't ask them questions that I couldn't answer. And I said, 'Why not? It's an important question. I'm just learning this stuff now, too, so we're going to figure it out together.' It was great."

By the end of the unit, Lisa was quite pleased with the learning that had occurred in her class—both her students' and her own.

> At the end of the fractions unit they were just beat. We had learned a lot about [fractions]. They were still pretty confused about why "of" means multiply, which is something I don't understand myself so I can't even help them. So these things are still issues. But they were thrilled with themselves when we got to decimals because within a week they understood almost all there was to know about them. They said to me, I can't believe this is so easy. And I said, that's because you were doing so much of your decimal work when you were doing fractions.

Establishing a Mathematics Community

At the beginning of the year, Lisa had worked to establish the idea that she and her students constituted a community engaged in a common process of inquiry. Yet, though her students had gotten used to collaborating in their other subjects, they did not automatically transfer these modes of interaction to their mathematics lessons. Prior classroom experience as well as deeply entrenched societal attitudes convey messages about what mathematics is and who can do it that often undermine the possibility of genuine community.

Among those messages, Lisa's students carried into her classroom the fundamental principle of traditional mathematics instruction: correct answers are the goal and confusion is shameful. Those students who had always been successful at rote computation were especially reluctant to change. They were used to being recognized as top students without making much of an effort and had no interest in taking on a challenge that might expose them as less than the best. Nor were the weaker students interested in engaging in a process that might render their coping mechanisms ineffective.

However, as Lisa persisted in asking probing questions, as she responded positively to the ideas her students offered, and as she consciously worked to create a safe environment, she soon persuaded her students that she expected every one of them to learn and to contribute.

"If the expectation that everyone is capable of understanding and solving the problem is established at the outset," she explained later, as she reviewed her year of instruction,

> [and] if kids are encouraged to debate and argue, to be wrong but interesting because it may be useful to the rest of the group as they struggle together with a problem (like why do you invert and multiply when dividing fractions?), they will persevere.

The inevitability of confusion, as well as the discomfort, became an acknowledged part of the ethos of the group:

> The old bugaboo [for me] remains division of fractions, which sometimes I understand, and at other times don't. This drives me crazy, since I never know when I'll get up to the blackboard with a kid to help with clarifying questions and then have to deal with internal white-out. The kids . . . call this process of disunderstanding "entering the Math Zone." When someone enters the Math Zone we all wax deeply sympathetic and hum in unison the Twilight Zone theme. This doesn't help any of us deal with the confusion engendered, but knowing that it is a recognizable place for most of us does lend the courage of camaraderie to what for me as a kid had always been a devastating and debilitating experience.

This recognition made possible the kind of learning that leads to the construction of powerful mathematical ideas.

> They understand that $\frac{1}{2}$ can be $\frac{1}{4}$ at the same time. [How did they learn that?] . . .They were motivated and excited by the ideas involved, and they weren't quite as scared as usual to be wrong because they had seen everyone, including myself, wrong. Because it was cool to be wrong as long as you're interesting!

Yet, even as this new atmosphere established itself in the classroom, Lisa became aware that some negative social norms continued to operate. Most dramatically, Lisa realized several months into the year, in this class of 8 girls and 15 boys, the girls had no voice. Gender patterns into which the children had been socialized in previous mathematics classrooms, patterns reinforced by societal attitudes, had become more obvious (Belenky, Clinchy, Goldberger, & Tarule, 1986; Chipman, Brush, & Wilson, 1985; Damarin, 1990; Fennema & Leder, 1990; Gilligan, 1982). Lisa had established a classroom dynamic of active and sometimes excited exchange of mathematical ideas, but the boys dominated discussion, while the girls, reticent about participating, were marginalized.

> The girls are very reluctant to compete with the boys. They are so afraid of being considered wrong and being made fun of. . . . it's the worst in math. They felt the worst about themselves mathematically.

Lisa saw a way to address the problem when, during a discussion with a mother who was concerned that her daughter had already given up on mathematics, Lisa suggested that the child stay after class on Wednesdays with a friend and do mathematics. But then, on second thought, why not encourage all eight girls to come? So the "girls' math club" was formed.

> We started out just doing what we were doing in class after school, and then we ended up getting there well before the rest of the class, and we ended up doing just lots of fun stuff . . . [There was always a] high level of noise and excitement. [They] would often solve problems while jumping up and down and singing. [I] brought the principal in a couple of times to witness this and to see long division and four-place multiplication in Xmanian. . . . I would have to throw them out at the end of an hour and a half. This is after a full day of school.

The formation of the girls' math club significantly altered the classroom dynamic.

> What the girls mastered . . . changed . . . their voice in the class. The voice of the classroom had been extremely masculine and what they did was to change the quality of that voice.

Rather than being intimidated into silence, the girls "came to realize the kinds of mistakes [they now saw] the boys were making . . . they'd been making [them] all along, but [the girls] hadn't been catching them."

The proactive intervention of the girls' math club was, in this case, necessary to counter the self-defeating attitudes that these girls had already developed about themselves and their mathematics ability.

Students' Responses to Mathematics Class

As a combination fifth- and sixth-grade teacher, Lisa taught some students two years in a row—both in the year prior to her participation in a SummerMath for Teachers institute and in her first year of active involvement. This provided an opportunity to explore these students' perspectives on how Lisa's mathematics instruction had changed. As it turned out, four boys—Ivan, Adam, Jacob, and Alex—and two girls—Lelieta and Ogechi—volunteered to be interviewed. Ivan and Adam had had Lisa for both fifth and sixth grades. Although the interviews were conducted in pairs, for the sake of readability the comments of all six students have been consolidated here into one discussion.

Interviewer: Ivan and Adam, did the way Ms. Yaffee taught math change from one year to the next?

Ivan: Yeah. Last year we just kept working in a book on our own. She didn't assign us pages. We just kept going on our own.

Adam: This year we learned a lot more. We learned why the problems worked, why the method worked. Last year we just did the stuff. If there was something new, like how to multiply fractions, Ms. Yaffee just told us, or the book did. It wouldn't ever say why.

Ivan: With math books we'd just learn the same basic things over and over again, but maybe the numbers would be a little bigger or harder. What we're learning now is a lot more complicated.

Adam: With the textbook, we'd just go through the book and we didn't really go over what we needed to know. Ms. Yaffee this year would give us a worksheet she made up, or we'd discuss it, and then she'd see how we'd do and if we looked like we needed . . . to know [more] then we'd start a section on that.

Interviewer: What about the rest of you. Was math class different for you than in past years?

Lelieta: It's a lot funner because it's not boring.

Ogechi: In previous years we really didn't ask questions. If you didn't know how to do problems in the book, [the teacher would] show you again and again until you knew how to do it and you could do it. You were supposed to memorize, This is right; this is wrong; do this, don't do that. You're supposed to do it this way.

Jacob: [Now] you have a problem and you do it one way, and [Ms. Yaffee] wants to know why you do it that way, why you chose it.

Ogechi: Sometimes if we didn't get it, we'd go over to other students who got it and if we didn't get it from them then we'd ask Ms. Yaffee and she'd try to make us understand by putting it in a different form. She didn't tell us why it works. Maybe she'd give you an example of some sort and from an example you might figure out why it works.

Lelieta: [When we could answer our own questions] we were excited about learning this new thing. It's a whole 'nother world.

Interviewer: I understand that you usually worked in groups. What was that like?

Adam: It's good to work in groups because when you get older you'll have to work in groups to get something done. How to cooperate and let other people talk.

Alex: By working in groups we also hear other people's point of view on the things, and hear things that we couldn't think of by working alone.

Ogechi: I like this year's math a lot better 'cause one of the main things is that last year there weren't any discussions.

Interviewer: You mean discussions in your small groups?

Ogechi: Yeah. But also with the whole class.

Alex: This year it gave us a chance to express our feelings about some of the problems and if we didn't understand we could get it cleared up. But not the answer. Other people's opinions.

Interviewer: What were the discussions like?

Lelieta: In group discussion, Ms. Yaffee asks the questions and sometimes the kids ask each other questions: How can you prove this works? Can I see how you prove this? Clarify how you prove this because I don't understand. How did you come up with this?

Jacob: We had a lot of conflicts.

Interviewer: How were conflicts resolved when students had different points of view?

Ogechi: [To decide if something's right or wrong] we'll have arguments between people. Then we'll find out . . . if it's a reasonable answer. [Sometimes it turns out] both of the persons are right.

Alex: Another way to see if a method is wrong is applying the method on whatever problems we're doing. Like, we have word problems every week. If someone suggests a method then we use that method and if we can apply it to the problems that we're doing and it doesn't work with what we're doing [then it's wrong].

Interviewer: You've talked a lot about how the class was different and how you understand things better. What about the math itself? Was what you studied any different?

Jacob: What we're doing now, making banquet tables out of squares [an activity Lisa had taken from Shroyer & Fitzgerald, 1986]. That's different. . . . Here we can see how with the same area you can make the perimeter bigger by changing the shape of the rectangle. In the book, it just says area is this and perimeter is this. But she does things like find the biggest perimeter and the smallest perimeter using 12 squares.

Alex: [And for fractions] we'd have to figure out a rule. We'd do these problems over and over again until we could see a rule and why it works. . . . We'd get math sheets with three pages and they'd be all different word problems and then we'd talk about what we did and then we'd talk about why something works. We'd just have to figure it out by doing the problems.

Jacob: Once we got through fractions and stuff, all of us understood numbers well enough that we could do the rest of the math things really easily. . . . Fractions is about understanding numbers and once we understood numbers we could do everything else really easily.

Alex: Another thing that's good this year is that Ms. Yaffee doesn't already know [a lot of the math]. She's just like one of the students. She just asks questions. She doesn't know the answers. She doesn't really know so it's not like she's superior to us.

Lelieta: When [Ms. Yaffee] was growing up she didn't know why you subtract when you do long division. People just told her to do it.

Ivan: She knows more now, though. And [next year] it will be not as good because then she'll know the answers so it won't be as good because there won't be so many arguments.

Ogechi: I think both us and her have learned a lot this year. . . . And I think . . . the class won't be as good next year because we're feeling that the teacher isn't that much more superior. She knew, but she didn't understand.

Adam: I hope next year in seventh grade math will be the same as Ms. Yaffee did it.

Lisa's Reflections

The changes in Lisa's mathematics instruction grew primarily out of her developing understanding of the discipline itself. In contrast to most other teachers who entered the program, Lisa began with a well-developed understanding of constructivism that formed the basis of her instruction in other subjects. Her colleague, Jill, was more typical, starting the school year with the idea that she wanted to use some new strategies in her classes, so her main task became to understand student learning in mathematics as a developmental process. Another colleague, Sherry, struggled with contradictions between equally compelling but very different conceptions of teaching, and unless she got some new classroom strategies working, the bigger questions would never get sorted out. [The stories of Jill and Sherry are told in other chapters of *Reconstructing Mathematics Education.*] But Lisa began with a strong sense of what her mathematics class should be like, and she already knew how to pay close attention to her students' learning. What she needed most was help in exploring mathematical issues related to the upper elementary curriculum. She also needed to develop confidence in her own power as a mathematical thinker.

> [Last summer] I was panicked and really upset because I knew I couldn't go back to doing what I had done. [But the institute] didn't give me the real basic practical stuff I needed. Then Deborah started coming on Wednesdays. I could say to her, How do you teach this? How do you teach that? What would you do about this? What would you do about that? And she had really concrete suggestions and materials. When I'd be leading my first tentative discussions and I didn't know what to say anymore, I'd just be standing there, but I could throw it to her and she would sort of lead me out of the mire. . . . So that's what changed it. Follow-up.

> What I loved about it was, there was no agenda. It was math therapy. I could go in and go, Oh my God, what do I do about this? I'm really confused about this. Someone asked me this question and I can't answer it. And whatever my agenda was, was the agenda. And that was great.

> Then she would say to me, Here are some problems. Why don't you look over them in your spare time? And I would. And I'd come back and say, I couldn't understand this, and we'd discuss it. And I could say things to her like, Well, what is the theory about this? It was like having a journal, but a journal with clarification, you know.

When Lisa was interviewed at the end of the year, she gave her overall sense of how things were going: "I do feel like it's working. I do, and I feel that next year

I'll know more about what I'm doing." Then she described how she had changed from September to June.

I'm a lot less nervous. I'm a little more confident, not a whole lot more confident. I'm only beginning to think mathematically now. I'm very shaky at it. For me [confidence as a mathematician and confidence as a math teacher] are very closely related.

When her interviewer told Lisa that her students felt she would never be as good a math teacher again because this was the year that she was learning along with her students, she responded:

I understand perfectly well that I can teach math well without understanding math. . . . I learned to use my not knowing to work for me. . . . But I don't like it. I feel like I could ask much better questions and write much better problems if I had a clearer understanding of what's involved. [My not understanding] limits a lot of what I can do.

"Besides," she said, "I have a lot more math to learn." When Lisa applied for another mathematics course offered by the program the following year, she listed some of the topics she now wanted to study:

I need to understand ratios, and how they differ conceptually from fractions. I need to be able to create a meaningful context for exponents, in addition to a better concept of their nature (including negative exponents and fractional ones). I need a better understanding of what negative numbers are. An exploration of how to define variables and how to use them would be useful, as would some context for graphing functions. I would love some theoretical background on what mathematics is, according to "them what knows." I've heard terms like "function," "relations," and so forth. What do they mean? My background in geometry is abysmal. What is it? What good is it? Why is space considered a mathematical entity? . . . What are trig. and calculus and why were they invented? Why is something raised to the 0 power one instead of zero?

"I'll tell you, Deborah," she wrote to the instructor, "you've got your work cut out for you."

What Did Lisa Know?

A point made repeatedly in this book is that, in order to be able to teach mathematics for "understanding" in the sense argued for here, teachers must know more mathematics than they, or most of their fellow citizens, currently do. Yet, Lisa's story poses a paradox. On the one hand, Lisa candidly admitted that she did not fully understand the mathematics she taught and frequently set problems for her students that she herself could not solve. On the other hand, she had become an unusually effective mathematics teacher. Her students could describe the ways in which their own mathematical understanding had improved and could even identify what Lisa had done to bring that understanding about. In fact, they believed that Lisa was a more effective teacher precisely because she didn't know the mathematics beforehand.

Resolution of this paradox lies in an appreciation of what Lisa did, in fact, bring to her mathematics instruction.

First, and perhaps most important, Lisa began with an appreciation of what it means to really learn something—"how to ask questions, and how to think about the questions you ask." Once she had confirmed subjectively, in her own struggles in the institute and in her work with Deborah, the relevance to mathematics of her theory of learning, she was able to overcome the paralysis that had affected her mathematics instruction. She decided that, just as she had done in other subject areas, so in her mathematics lessons she would aim to help her students learn to pose their own questions and would give them ways to think them through. She decided, too, to eschew pretense and use her own ignorance in order to model this process for them. By inviting her students to help her with her own questions, she could show them how to listen to others' ideas and demonstrate to them the value of collective inquiry.

But, in addition to her constructivist orientation, it is important to think about the mathematics Lisa knew. Here an analogy may be helpful: the teacher as guide. Leading her students into terrain unfamiliar to them and only imperfectly understood by her, she did have a map that identified at least some of this region's major topographical features. In order to begin to fill in the map—of fractions, for example—Lisa scouted some of the main concepts by herself, first with Deborah's help and then in the spring course. Through this work she was able to survey the overall terrain. She understood that among the major areas she needed to explore with her students were equivalent fractions, addition and subtraction with like denominators, addition and subtraction with unlike denominators, multiplication, and division. She also identified some of the big ideas that defined the geological substructure of the region: that the same object can represent fractions of different values, depending on the reference whole; that the referent remains constant when one is adding or subtracting, but changes when one is multiplying or dividing; that some generalizations about whole-number operations (e.g., a product is almost always larger than its factors; a quotient is almost always smaller than its dividend) no longer hold; that the very meanings of multiplication and division must be extended beyond the meanings derived from whole-number operations.

All this enabled Lisa to select a route—to write word-problem sets—that would lead her students to the high ground from which they could view the surrounding terrain. She understood, too, that in order to monitor her students' developing maps so as to determine which trails to take next and where they needed to explore further, she had to listen carefully to their ideas and challenge them to articulate those ideas clearly. Lisa had to distinguish valid arguments from invalid ones, lead her students through their misconceptions when they wandered from the trail, and even fill in swampy ground to make it traversable.

With these kinds of knowledge and understandings, Lisa could design lessons and conduct classes in ways that enabled her students to construct their own internal maps of fractions country. That did not mean, however, that she needed to have already charted for herself each trail her students would need to go down, each obstacle they would encounter. It did mean that she had to be prepared to acknowledge that she, too, had lost her way, that she had more exploring to do. "At times," Lisa said,

> I would be confused; I would make mistakes; and I would not know what I was doing. And the kids could clearly see that. I would become confused over a problem that I didn't really understand. . . . There was a division-of-decimals problem *[Tali weighs 61 pounds. If his weight is .80 of his best friend's, how much does Tali's friend weigh?]* that I had written that I didn't understand. . . . Alex, Jacob, and Lelieta understood it and I didn't, and they knew that. And I said to them, I can't understand this, so I'm just going to have to work on it myself.

Though Lisa was candid about the limits of her own understanding, her students did not lose respect for her. They recognized that she was being honest with them, and, by the example she set, they learned that it was not shameful to admit ignorance. Through her own efforts to understand the mathematical ideas, Lisa communicated the importance of what they were learning.

Lisa's students could see that she often did not understand the mathematics they were learning, but they also knew that they were not wandering aimlessly: the lessons were organized and focused. They trusted Lisa to guide them, and their awareness of the power of their own learning—when they looked back down the trail they could see the progress they had made—reinforced that trust.

Thus, the question is not whether Lisa understood all the mathematics she was teaching, but rather, What did Lisa know that, in spite of the gaps in her understanding, made her so effective?

This chapter has described Lisa's struggle to generalize the patterns she discovered in the multiplication and division of fractions problems she worked on. For example, to solve one of those problems (Marissa bought 0.46 . . .), she first estimated that the answer was close to or just over one half, and then calculated the result, .55. Yet she wrote, "I knew it was a division problem but I couldn't explain why. . . . [I want to know] what the problem is about at its core."

And though some of her students were able to solve the problem about Tali's friend's weight, Lisa insisted that she herself didn't understand the crux of the problem. But her confessions of ignorance need not be taken at face value. After all, she had written that problem in order to explore division of decimals, and she had solved it. But it was something else she was after—"What is it in these problems that makes them division problems?"—and, though she didn't yet understand that, it was she who had helped Alex, Jacob, and Lelieta to see further, at that moment, than she herself was able to see.

By posing that question to the class—"What makes these division problems?"— she did more for them than untold hours of mechanical practice at an algorithm could have accomplished. For in listening carefully to her students' ideas, she validated the power of their thinking. And by working at the edge of her own mathematical understanding, Lisa not only enlarged her students' opportunities for learning, but she provided herself the best possible setting for the kind of learning she needed to do and now knew she was capable of.

References

Belenky, M. F., Clinchy, B. N., Goldberger, N. R., & Tarule, J. M. (1986). *Women's ways of knowing.* New York: Basic Books.

Chipman, S. F., Brush, L. R., & Wilson, D. M. (1985). *Women and mathematics: Balancing the equation.* Hillsdale, NJ: Lawrence Erlbaum Associates.

Damarin, S. K. (1990). Teaching mathematics: A feminist perspective. In T. J. Cooney & C. R. Hirsch (Eds.), *Teaching and learning mathematics in the 1990's* (pp. 144–151). Reston, VA: National Council of Teachers of Mathematics.

Driscoll, M. (1983). *Research within reach: Secondary school mathematics—A research guided response to the concerns of educators.* Reston, VA: National Council of Teachers of Mathematics.

Fennema, E., & Leder, G. C. (Eds.) (1990). *Mathematics and gender.* New York: Teachers College Press.

Gilligan, C. (1982). *In a different voice.* Cambridge, MA: Harvard University Press.

Harel, G., Behr, M., Post, T., & Lesh, R. (1989). *Teachers' knowledge of multiplication and division concepts.* Unpublished manuscript.

Owens, D. T. (1988). Understanding decimal multiplication in grade six. In M. J. Behr, C. B. Lacampagne, & M. M. Wheeler (Eds.), *Proceedings of the Tenth Annual Meeting of the North American Chapter of the International Group for the Psychology of Mathematics Education* (pp. 107–113). Dekalb, IL: Northern Illinois University.

Shroyer, J., & Fitzgerald, W. (1986). *Mouse and elephant: Measuring growth.* Menlo Park, CA: Addison-Wesley.

Student Misconceptions and a Teacher's Long-Term Agenda

This section contains the transcript for a video clip that you view during the second session of *Lenses on Learning, Module 3*. The video shows a portion of Steve Walkowicz's sixth-grade class, with students working in groups and sharing their ideas for solving a single problem.

READING 3   "What Is 5% of 40?" (Mathematical Inquiry Through Video)

Like other videotapes shown in this seminar, this one offers a glimpse of what a standards-based mathematics class might look like. It gives you a chance to explore how children's mathematical thinking develops—and how misconceptions can arise—in the context of a percentage problem. Please remember that your purpose here is *not* to critique the teaching of Mr. Walkowicz, but rather to strive to understand the student thinking he is dealing with and to look for the underlying mathematical ideas.

You are asked to think about the following questions as you view the videotape a second time:

- What do you think was going on for the students who had misconceptions?

- What did Mr. Walkowicz need to know in order to make sense of the misconceptions students were expressing and help them move beyond those misconceptions?

- What kinds of moves did Mr. Walkowicz make in response to student errors, and how might they have reflected his long-term mathematical agenda?

As you discuss the video with other participants, this transcript will be a useful reference.

What Is 5% of 40?
Rewards and Pitfalls of Sharing Student Solutions
Mathematical Inquiry Through Video

Teacher: Steve [Walkowicz]
Total Time: 11 minutes
Tape Version: Final © 1997

Note: Reset your VCR time counter to zero when classroom footage begins.

00:00 [Mr. Walkowicz introduces the problem.]

[(Mr. Walkowicz) is at the front of the class referring to a problem on the blackboard.]

1   [Mr. Walkowicz]: It starts . . . you start with forty pennies. When you're done with number one and two. Most of you have no problem with that. Now it asks you to take five percent of the remaining pennies away. We gotta figure out what five percent of forty is. Take a minute and talk with your group about that right now. And see if you can figure out what forty perc . . . what five percent of forty is.

2   *[The students are working in groups at their desks. We hear general discussion before focusing in on Sida and Tim.]*

3   Boy: 8 percent.

4   Boy: No, no, no.

5   Boy: Eight.

6   Sida: [*shaking head*] Eight pennies.

7   Tim: Yeah.

8   Sida: [*unclear, possibly "eight pennies" said more slowly*]

9   Tim: Good job, Sida.

10 Sida: It's, it's eight pennies.

11 Tim: Yeah, eight pennies.

12   Sida: No, this, I still don't get this one [*repeatedly taps his finger on his paper*].

13   Tim: Which one?

14   Sida: Yeah. [*Sida agrees, possibly because Tim had nonverbally located the problem Sida was talking about.*]

15   Boy: [*unclear, possibly "I don't know . . ."*]

16   Tim: That one's harder.

17   [Mr. Walkowicz]: If you have an answer, if you have an answer just raise your hand.

18   Sida: OK.

19   [*Sida's and Tim's hands dart up. Jeremy, the other student in the group, half lifts his hand.*]

20   [Mr. Walkowicz]: OK. We've got one, two, three groups, four groups. We're still waiting on a couple here.

21   Sida: Watch, I'll continue to minus . . . [*Sida inputs a problem into his calculator and pauses to read the answer.*] . . . Six.

22   Tim: Is it?

23   Sida: Uh, but, I know what's . . . uh . . . minus.

~01:00   The class reports their answers.

24   [Mr. Walkowicz]: OK. Uh, let's see what we've got . . . Tim, what's your group have?

25   Tim: We have . . . five percent of forty is eight. Eight pennies.

26   Sida: Yeah, eigh . . . eigh . . . eight pennies.

27   [Mr. Walkowicz]: What, what do you guys have over here, now?

28   Other group: Eight [*unintelligible*].

29   Sida: [*to himself*] Eight pennies.

30   [Mr. Walkowicz]: You have eight. OK. What do you have over here, Andre?

31   [*We see a panoramic view of the room.*]

32   Andre: We have eight.

33   [Mr. Walkowicz]: You have eight.

34   Student: [*softly*] We have two.

35   Boy: Two . . .

36   [Mr. Walkowicz]: What do you have here? [*addresses Sean's table, the group sitting closest to him*]

37   Sean: Two.

38   [Mr. Walkowicz]: You have two. And you guys? [*points to Amanda's table*]

39   Amanda: Two.

40   [Mr. Walkowicz]: Two. And did you guys get an answer yet? [*pointing to table in far corner*]

41   Jean: Yep.

42   [Mr. Walkowicz]: What did you get?

43   Jean: Eight.

44   [Mr. Walkowicz]: So we have . . . Does anyone know what percent of the groups got eight?

45   Student: Uhm . . . [*very softly*] four out of six.

46   [Mr. Walkowicz]: We have four out of six, which is the same as two out of three, which is the same as what percent?

47   [*"E"'s hand flies up.*]

48   "E": Oh, sixty . . . six and seven [*unclear, but do hear an "er", so possibly "thirds"*].

49   [Mr. Walkowicz]: Sixty-six and two thirds percent, right?

50   "E": Yeah. Yeah.

~02:00 Felice explains how she got "2."

51   [Mr. Walkowicz]: OK. So it looks like eight's the answer, right? Somebody from the two . . . that got two, how'd you get two? Felice?

52   Felice: [*Felice is at her desk*] OK. Well I did, uhm, forty minus point-oh-five, and then I just subtracted it and I got two, zero, zero, and then move two places and you get two.

53   [*Amanda, sitting next to Felice, raises her hand as Felice finishes*]

54   [Mr. Walkowicz]: Could you show us? I, I didn't understand what you said [*hands chalk to Felice*]. I heard the word "minus" and I'm not quite sure where that comes in.

55   [*Felice goes to the board, writes "40 − .0_" then turns and softly asks her table mates a question.*]

56   Felice: What was the number?

57   Girl: [*unintelligible*]

58   Felice: Wait, what was the number . . . point-oh-what? [*her table mate says something unclear*] Wait, I need to get my paper.

59   [*Felice walks to her desk, looks at her paper and returns to the board.*]

60   [Mr. Walkowicz]: [*to another student*] OK. Well you can, you can, you can, uh . . .

61   [*At the board, Felice finishers her equation as follows:*]

$$\begin{array}{r} 40 \\ -\ .05 \\ \hline 2.00 \end{array}$$

Figure 1. Felice's explanation for the answer "2"

62   [*Felice turns, raises her hands as if to say, "That's all," and then returns to her seat.*]

~03:00 [Mr. Walkowicz] solicits questions about Felice's work.

63   [Mr. Walkowicz]: Look at what Felice did. Anyone have a question that they want to ask Felice?

64   Boy: Wait a second.

65   [Mr. Walkowicz]: Any questions about that?

66   Same boy: [*quietly*] Yeah . . .

67   [*Many hands are up.*]

68   [Mr. Walkowicz]: No, no questions? You'd, you'd accept that, Craig? That looks good?

69   Craig: [*softly*] I have something else. I have another . . .

70   [Mr. Walkowicz]: Any observations about what she's got up there, though?

71   Craig: [*lowers his arm and looks at board*] Mmm . . .

72   Sean: Uhmm . . . [*unclear, possibly, "I want to go up there."*] Mr. Walkowicz, can I show how I . . . ?

73   [Mr. Walkowicz]: [*inaudible name, possibly "Veron"*], what do you think? Let's look at what she did before we talk about what we did.

74   Veronica: [*across from Craig*] I don't really get it because . . . it seems like it's uh, it's, forty minus five and, . . . and well, I, I just don't really get what it means.

~03:30 Amanda's method for getting "2."

75   [Mr. Walkowicz]: Can anyone? Amanda, you were with . . . Felice, right?

76   Amanda: [*rises and goes to the board*] I did it kind of different. I did it as a fraction . . . instead of a . . . decimal. So I did . . .

77   [*Amanda draws two fraction lines on the board before writing any numbers.*]

78   Amanda: I did one hundred [*writes 100 in denominator of second fraction*] forty [*puts 40 in numerator above*]. Then I did five into one hundred goes twenty times and twenty times two is forty, so I got two.

79   [*Amanda turns to class after completing her problem as below:*]

$$\frac{2}{5} \quad \frac{40}{100}$$

Figure 2. Amanda's method for solving 5% of 40

80   Student: Yeah.

81   Amanda: 'Cause like . . .

82   [Mr. Walkowicz]: So you, you did it as a proportion?

83   Boy: [*softly*] So doesn't that . . . ?

84   Kevin: A proportion?

85   [Mr. Walkowicz]: Well, why, why . . .

86   "E": Oh, oh, oh, oh! [*raising his hand*]

87   Boy: Isn't like two-fifths like . . . point four?

88   [Mr. Walkowicz]: Yeah, "E", yours is the same group, right?

89   "E": Yeah [*goes to board*].

90   [Mr. Walkowicz]: I'm still, I'm still wondering about Felice, here. [*laughter*] I'm stuck on that because we can't go beyond that.

91   Student: [*inaudibly talks to (Mr. Walkowicz)*]

92   [Mr. Walkowicz]: Well, once I get unstuck on Felice, I'll wonder about Amanda's, too. Very interesting.

~04:30 "E"'s method

93   [*"E" writes the following on the board.*]

$$\begin{array}{r} 40 \\ \times\, .05 \\ \hline \end{array}$$

Figure 3. "E"'s method for getting "2"

94   [Mr. Walkowicz]: All right, "E", talk to us.

95   "E": OK.

96   [Mr. Walkowicz]: 'Cause that looks just like what Felice had only a little different.

97   Felice: Oh, oh, oh, wait! It's not supposed to be . . . I didn't even do mine, 'cause I did multiplication.

98   "E": Uhm, I did, uhm, forty percent, I did, I did five, five . . . [*sigh*] five percent of forty which is . . . "of" [*points to the multiplication sign in his equation*], is equal to, is the same thing as "times." And, uhm, so . . . five times zero is zero and then five times forty is two – is twenty and, uhm, there's two decimal points, and you move it over twice and you get two.

99   [*As he speaks he is finding his solution. He writes "2.00" under the equation in Figure 3.*]

100   [Mr. Walkowicz]: So you got two. What do you think of it, Felice?

101   Felice: OK, well, I did multiplication but I wrote a minus sign.

~05:30 [Mr. Walkowicz] asks for explanations of the answer "8."

102   [Mr. Walkowicz]: All right, so, so. You're OK. You're absolved. [*louder*] Now, how about someone who got an eight? [*Some hands are raised.*] Andre?

103   Andre: I didn't really need to [*inaudible*] but . . . I just, uh, found a number that . . . well, eight goes into "forty" five times.

104   [Mr. Walkowicz]: So you said . . . you were thinking of some number that goes into forty five times.

105   Andre: Yeah. Eight.

~06:00 Sean's method for getting "2."

106   [Mr. Walkowicz]: All right. Sean.

107   Sean: [*immediately rises and goes to the board*] I got two but, what I did was . . . [*walks to the board*] I found, first I found ten percent of forty which is four [*writes 4*] and then half, uhm, five percent is half, five is half of ten so you would divide this in, in half which would be two. Because five percent is half of ten percent. So if ten percent is four then it would be two.

108   [Mr. Walkowicz]: So, so you're, you're with the group here that says it's two?

109   Sean: Yeah.

110   [Mr. Walkowicz]: OK.

111   Tim: Can we change our answer?

112   [Mr. Walkowicz]: Can I get one more person with the eights and who, who is still convinced that eight is the right answer. 'Cause I, I'm hearing Tim say he wants to change his answer. Nick . . . [*points across the room*].

113   Nick: That's all we did.

114   [Mr. Walkowicz]: You think that that's the right thing to do in this case?

115   Nick: I guess so.

116   [Mr. Walkowicz]: Huh?

117   Nick: Yeah.

118   [Mr. Walkowicz]: You still think so? Yeah?

119   Nick: Yeah.

120   Kevin: I don't think . . . [*strikes the table and looks at Nick, who's in his group*] Not.

~07:00 Nate explains the answer "8."

121   [Mr. Walkowicz]: OK. Uhm . . . Nate.

122   Nate: [*inaudible*] . . . blank equals forty and blank is eighty. I did, like, I did, uhm, forty divided by five is eight. So I got, uhm, and that's how I got eight.

123   [Mr. Walkowicz]: OK. Let, let me, let me just try something here [*goes to the board*]. I'm hearing people saying that they had forty left and they're supposed to take five percent of it. So they're thinking, "Five goes into forty . . . eight times," so it must be you could take eight away, right?

124   [*Writes the following on the board:*]

$$5 \overline{)\, 40} \quad \text{(quotient } 8)$$

Figure 4. [Mr. Walkowicz] summarizes one method for getting the answer "8."

~07:30 [Mr. Walkowicz] suggests a test.

125   [Mr. Walkowicz]: How about if you had to take forty percent of forty away? Instead of taking five percent away, let's say it was forty percent away. Now you've got forty pennies. You're going to divide 'em by forty . . . and you're going to get . . . one?

126   [*Writes the following on the board:*]

$$40 \overline{)\, 40} \quad \text{(quotient } 1)$$

Figure 5. [Mr. Walkowicz] tests the 'divide 5 into 40' method.

127   [Mr. Walkowicz]: Is for . . ., is forty percent of forty, one?

128   Students: No.

129   [Mr. Walkowicz]: Or how 'bout if it was fifty percent of the remaining pennies away.

130   [*(Mr. Walkowicz) changes his last division problem to 40 divided by 50.*]

131   [Mr. Walkowicz]: Do you divide that by fifty, and get four-fifths?

132   Student: No. You get thirty.

~08:00 Sida changes his answer.

133   [Mr. Walkowicz]: Is that. I don't know if that confuses you more. Sida?

134   Sida: Uhm, our group got eight, for the answer. But I think it should be really two. 'Cause we did it wrong 'cause, uhm, it should be five percent. And . . . once we change it to a decimal it should be point-oh-five instead of point five which will be a half. And then you multiply it by a forty.

135   [Mr. Walkowicz]: OK. So, so th . . . change this . . . we change this to a decimal. You could change it to a fraction if you wanted to call it one-twentieth [*writes on the board*]. And then you multiply it by forty and you're going to get "two" as an answer. So, you're taking two pennies away, how many are left? So that the twos are right.

~09:00 Craig's strategy for getting "2."

136   [Mr. Walkowicz]: Craig?

137   Craig: I just wanted to say that I have, I have another strategy to find out two. I, I want to . . . can I come up?

138   Craig: [*at the board*] I figured five percent equals, like, one-twentieth 'cause five goes into a hundred, uhm, twenty times, so it's, so one-twentieth. So, so . . . it would equal two, because, two . . . one . . . twenty goes into it two times and you times the one by two and you get two. So, that's the answer.

139   [Mr. Walkowicz]: So you're taking one-twentieth of what?

140   Craig: What?

141   [Mr. Walkowicz]: You're taking one-twentieth of . . . ?

142   Craig: Of forty.

143   [Mr. Walkowicz]: Forty.

144   Craig: Yeah.

145   [Mr. Walkowicz]: You did all that in your head?

146   Craig: Yeah.

147   [Mr. Walkowicz]: So, if we are taking . . . if we're trying to find a percent OF something, one way you . . . is to change it to a . . . [*points to Craig*]

148   Craig: Fraction.

149   [Mr. Walkowicz]: Fraction or a ratio, right. Which you just did. And another way is to do what? If you want to find a percent of a number? Like five percent of forty? He turned it to one-twentieth. That's one really good way. Another way is . . . [*points to another student*].

150   Student: Change it to a decimal?

151   [Mr. Walkowicz]: Change it to a decimal. Right.

~10:00 The End

A Teacher Puzzling Over Pedagogical Choices

During the third session of *Lenses on Learning, Module 3,* you watch a video clip that offers a peek into Sherry Sajdak's sixth-grade classroom. The following reading is a transcript for that clip.

READING 4   "Area and Perimeter: Student Confusions" (Mathematical Inquiry Through Video)

As you watch this video clip, you will be trying to figure out the teacher's intent for a particular lesson (in this case, a lesson involving area and perimeter). You will also be trying to make sense of the student confusions brought out by that lesson, and you will be thinking about ways the teacher may want to revise her instructional plan after learning from her students how complicated this topic is for them.

This can be a challenging video to discuss because the students' discourse moves quickly and is not easy to follow. The transcript is provided so that you can return to particular lines to make better sense of what the students are saying. During discussion, you can also use the transcript to find examples to illustrate your points.

After a second viewing of the video, you will be discussing these questions:

- What powerful mathematical ideas do you think Ms. Sajdak had hoped to address with this activity?

- What do the students understand and what are they confused about?

- If Ms. Sajdak left this class puzzling about her long-term mathematical agenda, what do you think she was wondering about?

Area and Perimeter: Student Confusions

Mathematical Inquiry Through Video

Teacher: Sherry [Sajdak]
Total Time: 18 minutes
Tape Version: Final © 1997

Note: Reset your VCR time counter to zero when classroom footage begins.

00:00 [Ms. Sajdak] introduces the lesson.

1   [Ms. Sajdak]: How many of you feel . . . comfortable with a rectangle that has a whole number and another number with a half? Be, be honest, you feel comfortable?

2   [*Many students raise their hands.*]

3   [Ms. Sajdak]: Mike? Sort of like?

4   Mike: Sort of maybe . . .

5   [Ms. Sajdak]: Sort of? OK. I'm going to give you a problem that has a half for the side edge, a half in the number, and a half in the, on the bottom edge. I would like you and your partner to work through the problem . . . and discuss all the parts of it. Now you may have a different way of doing the problem than your partner does. So you need to talk about the ways to solve the problem. Shake your heads if you understand what I mean.

6   [*Visible students shake their heads, "yes."*]

7   [Ms. Sajdak]: OK. All right. So . . . I think I am going to give you . . . The bottom edge is going to be four and a half units and for the side edge it's going to be six and a half units.

Find the area and perimeter [of a rectangle] if the bottom edge is $4\frac{1}{2}$ units and side edge is $6\frac{1}{2}$ units.

Figure 1. The problem [Ms. Sajdak] gave her students to work in class.

~1:15 Dropping in on Shaina, Ellen, and Mark . . .

8 Shaina: Uhm . . . right. Uhm. . .

9 Ellen: [*very softly*] Do we need . . . graph paper?

10 Shaina: All right. Let's make the . . . let's try and make the four and a half first on the bottom, right?

11 Ellen: [*says something that can't be understood*]

12 [*heard in the background*]

13 [Ms. Sajdak]: Sarah? Danny's your partner?

14 Sarah: Yeah.

15 [Ms. Sajdak]: So you two are [*inaudible*].

16 Sarah: Yeah.

17 [*in the foreground again*]

18 [*Shaina looks expectantly at Ellen*]

19 Ellen: I don't know.

20 Shaina: So let's try and make the four and a half on the bottom.

21 Ellen: Yeah, so we start . . . That's the bottom, right there?

22 Shaina: [*counting and drawing*] . . . two, . . .

23 Ellen: OK.

24 Shaina: [*still drawing*] . . . three . . . All right, that works, I think.

25 Ellen: OK.

26 Shaina: But 1, 2, 3, 4 and a half . . . 1, 2 . . . Wait a minute. But these are halves, so you have to count them as one.

27 Ellen: Yeah. [*unclear*] So if we went [*starting at the arrow (figure 2), counts by twos*] there's a whole, there's a whole, here's a whole. . .

28 Shaina: Three . . .

29 Ellen: . . . and then there's an odd number [*at the pencil*].

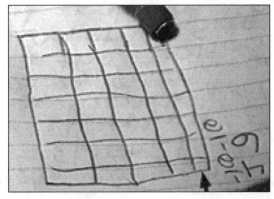

Figure 2. Starting at the arrow, Ellen combines "half" squares into wholes, concluding "and then there's an odd number" (at her pencil).

30   Shaina: [*continuing her running count*] . . . three and a half.

~2:00 "It's an odd number! It's a confuse number."

31   Shaina: All right. Let's start from the beginning again. All right. [*shades the "halves" column in her new drawing, on graph paper, Figure 3*]

32   Ellen: All right, and then Mark had the idea where we put the . . . four and a half on the bottom. Right here . . . [*extends the vertical edge of the rectangle down a half unit and draws a new horizontal edge, Figure 3*]

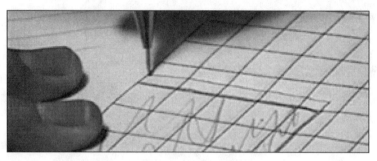

Figure 3. Ellen draws the bottom row of "half" squares.

33   Shaina: Mm hmm. All right.

34   Ellen: So it's like this . . .

35   Shaina: Wait a minute!

36   Ellen: . . . and then you see two of these is a whole, so here's a one whole . . . [*pointing with pencil to a square above the row of "half" squares just drawn*], then . . . [*marks off "2" with pencil*] . . . here is the—[*pointing at the quarter square*] . . . You see, it's an odd number! It's a confuse number.

37   Shaina: We have . . . [*combining the "half" squares along the vertical edge of the rectangle*] one, two, three and a half. 1, 2 [*combining half squares along base*] Let's just, let's forget about those two [*covering the corner one-fourth of a square with finger*]. 3, 4 . . . [*counting whole squares within rectangle in one breath*] 5, 6, 7, 8, 9, 10, 11, 12, 13, 14, 15, 16, 17, 18, 19, 20, 21, 22, 23, 24, 25, 26, 27, 28. Twenty-eight and a half is what I've got for the area.

38   Ellen: Yeah, but we can't have that other half [*overlapping with Shaina*]. Doesn't it have to be a whole?

39   Shaina: I know. How do ya get rid of that though?

40   Ellen: Well . . . I gotta think.

~3:00 [Mark joins the debate.]

41   Shaina: That's a half.

42   Ellen: I know this is a half. You got it?

43   Shaina: [*pointing isn't visible*] That's a half, and that's a half, so we put those together and we have twenty-nine. Perimeter is twenty-three and the area is twenty-nine.

44   Mark: [*offscreen*] I got twenty.

45   Shaina: Let's check on our thing again. One . . .

46   [*scene shifts as she counts squares*]

47   Shaina: 1, 2, 3, 4, and $\frac{1}{2}$.

48   Ellen: [*to Mark*] Twenty? How'd you get . . .

49   Shaina: [*also to Mark*] Twenty is what?—as what?

50   Mark: Twenty is the perimeter.

51   Shaina: How'd ya get 20 as the perimeter?

52   Mark: Counted. I . . . first I added it all, then I just counted to make sure. See?

53   Ellen: [*counting each edge of a half square on Mark's paper as if it is a half-length unit*] 1, 2, 3 [*up the side*] . . . 4, 5 [*across bottom*].

54   Shaina: No, no, no, wait a minute. You're counting wrong. These [*each edge of a half square*] count as one thing [*for the perimeter*]. Here, hold on. These count as one thing.

55   Mark: See? 1, 2, 3, 4, 5, 6 [*counting the length units at the vertical edge of the rectangle, Figure 4*].

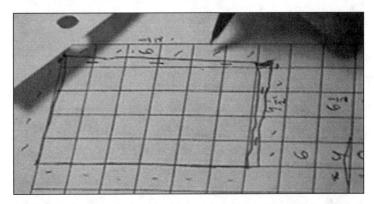

Figure 4. Mark counts the length of the vertical edge made up of six half units.

56   Shaina: 1, 2, 3 . . . 4, 5, 6. [*repeating Mark's counting procedure on her own paper*] That counts as six.

57   Ellen: Mark [*inaudible*]

58   Shaina: 'Cause that's [*points to unit length, arrow 1, Figure 5-A*] the same thing as this. [*traces equivalent length at arrow 2*]

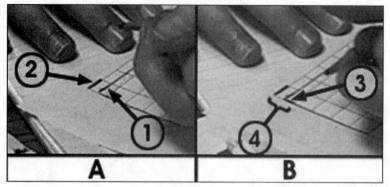

Figure 5. Shaina traces over lines, comparing the sides of the corner half-square.

59   Shaina: But going around the corner [*traces half unit at arrow 3, Figure 5-B*], it's not the same width as THIS [*extending the line to the width of a whole unit, bracket 4*]. So you have to count this as a half [*at arrow 3*] and this [*half at other end*] as a half, but the rest is all wholes.

~4:00 Moving to another table: Josh and Sarah.

60   Josh: [*counting around the edges of the rectangle he's drawn, Figure 6*] Sixteen . . . skip over those two [*edges of corner quarter square*] . . . 17, 18, 19, 20 . . .

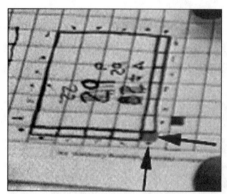

Figure 6. Josh counts the perimeter of his $4\frac{1}{2} \times 6\frac{1}{2}$ rectangle, " . . . skip over those two . . ."

61   Sarah: [*reaches to point at Josh's paper*]

62   Josh: That's one . . .

63   Sarah: This [*pointing to the sides of the quarter square*] is a fourth and a fourth . . . it equals a half . . .

64   Josh: . . . it's a half.

65   Sarah: But, it's not straight. It would equal, it would equal . . .

66   Josh: See, it's halfway down and halfway across.

67   Sarah: [*sighs with some frustration*] It would equal a whole if it was straight, but it's not straight. So it's a half.

68   Josh: I don't get what you're saying.

69   Sarah: You don't get it?

70   Josh: You got a line coming this way . . .

71   Sarah: Yeah.

72   Josh: . . . and that's . . .

73   Sarah: . . . a fourth . . . and here's a fourth. What do two fourths equal?

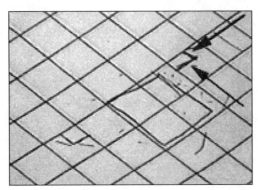

Figure 7. Sarah adds the length of the two sides of the controversial fraction of a square.

74   Josh: A half.

75   Sarah: YES!

76   Josh: But it's not fourths. See. This is [*unclear*] . . .

~4:30 Sarah asserts, "The half is straight here . . . you can sit a person there."

77   Sarah: But, see, if . . . [*sighs*]

78   Josh: [*very softly*] Look, look.

79   Sarah: . . . see, the half is straight here [*referring to the long edge of the half square*].

80   Josh: Mm hmm.

81   Sarah: It's equal, see . . . like that. See, they're both equal to that because they're straight and you can like sit a person there [*at arrow, Figure 8*] if they were tables.

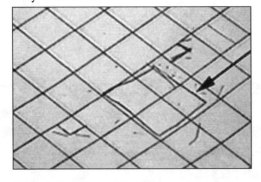

Figure 8. Sarah says, "The half is straight here."

82   Sarah: But see, with this . . . part of the person goes here and part of the person goes there [*see arrows, Figure 9*]. [*Sarah ends with a frustrated, voiced sigh.*]

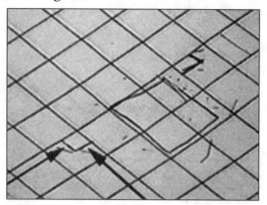

Figure 9. ". . . part of the person goes here [at one arrow] and part of the person goes there [at the other arrow]."

83   Josh: But we're not talking tables.

84   Sarah: It doesn't matter.

85   Josh: I can still count it as a half, though.

86   Sarah: Let me show you, again. See like this, there's a fourth here, and a fourth here. [*referring to two sides of quarter square in Figure 10*] And here [*at the arrow in Figure 10*] there's one, but it's still a half, but it's counted as one because a whole person can sit on this edge. Here, there's two parts of the person that has to sit two parts of the table.

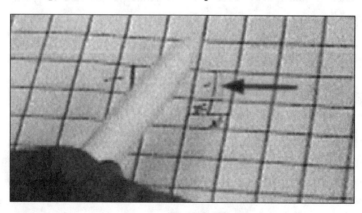

Figure 10. Sarah draws another illustration. "And here there's one, but it's still a half, but it's counted as one . . ."

87   [*Sarah pauses to look at Josh, then sighs audibly, putting her head in her hand.*]

88   Sarah: [*softly motioning toward Mary*] Do you get what I'm saying?

89   Mary: [*pointing to her paper and finishing what she was saying*] . . . we haven't even done the perimeter yet.

90   Mary: [*nodding in answer to Sarah*] Yeah.

91   Josh: All right, going around this whole squ . . ., uh, whole rectangle, and if, if you're gonna go around it, you're gonna have to uhm, you're gonna have to count the, the side edge and the bottom edge together.

92   Mary: Josh, it's like this. Even though this is half a table [*apparently pointing to corner quarter square*], a person still sits there, not—a whole person, not a half a person.

~6:00 The debate continues.

93   Sarah: See? See with this part [*pointing to a half square along the base*], you counted this as one because it's a full edge [*traces the long edge*]. But here, this p . . . [*pointing to corner quarter square*], this end and this end only equal a half.

94   Josh: But we're not talking people.

95   Sarah: It doesn't matter. [*She laughs.*]

96   Josh: You're going half . . .

97   Sarah: We could be using ears for all I care.

98   Josh: You're going halfway, you're going this way, the bottom edge [*of corner quarter*], you're going halfway, going that way [*the vertical edge*], so you add them both together and you get a whole.

99   Sarah: Nooo, this is a fourth and this is a fourth. They equal a half.

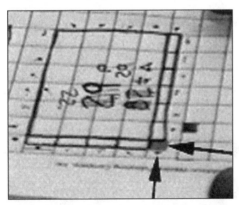

Figure 11. "This is a fourth and this is a fourth. They equal a half," says Sarah, referring to the sides of the corner square at arrows.

100 Josh: Can I, can I tell you something? It's a fourth, it's a fourth going downward, I mean it's a half going downward. Because you're going downward and it's halfway down. But when you're going "across," it's halfway across too. So it's not equal as a fourth.

101 Sarah: [*whispering*] Yes it is. [*louder*] It's a fourth of a PIECE.

~7:00 Whole-class discussion

102 [Ms. Sajdak]: So I would like to know if somebody would like, a group, you and your partner or partners . . .

103   Danny: [*turning to Caitlin behind him, says softly*] Do you want to go up? [*Caitlin nods yes.*]

104   [Ms. Sajdak]: . . . would like to volunteer to come up to the board to explain . . . explain, [*Danny and Caitlin raise their hands*] uhm, how you did the problem. So I need . . . so Caitlin and Danny. 'Cause I need to see both hands of the partners. Your eyes should be on task.

105   [*Danny and Caitlin go to board. Caitlin draws their diagram on large graph paper taped to the board.*]

106   [Ms. Sajdak]: And Danny, since she's drawing, could you tell everybody what she's doing?

107   Danny: She's drawing this up here [*points to word problem on the board*].

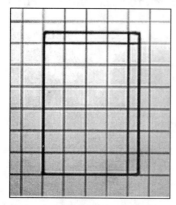

Figure 12. Caitlin's drawing places the "half" squares along the top and the right side.

~7:30 "We're going to explain about the 'halfs' . . ."

108   Danny: [*not looking at Caitlin's drawing*] And we're going to explain about the "halfs" . . . from the bottom side and the side . . . and the uh . . . from the bottom part and the side part . . .

109   [*Danny now draws on graph paper.*]

110   Danny: When you're, uh . . . count . . . [*writes along the right-hand length of rectangle*] these two as one [*brackets them together*] and these two as one, and these two.

111   [Ms. Sajdak]: What about on the other side, what are you counting?

112   Danny: Count . . . right here? [*repositions marker to left side and looks at (Ms. Sajdak)*] You count that as one, that one . . . [*labels left edge with six "1's"*] like that. You count each one as one. Except for right there . . . that's a half [*writes "$\frac{1}{2}$" alongside the top left half-square*].

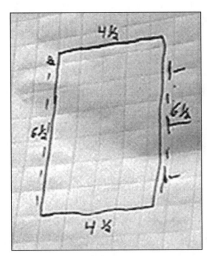

Figure 13. Danny counts along both sides of the rectangle.

113	[Ms. Sajdak]: And what are you counting again?
114	Danny: The . . . perimeter
115	[Ms. Sajdak]: The perimeter. So what d'ya think? . . . Mark.
116	Caitlin: Well, this is kinda confusing [*drops voice to inaudible level*].
117	[Ms. Sajdak]: There's something . . . there's something puzzling you here.
118	Caitlin: Yeah.
119	[Ms. Sajdak]: So Ashley, can you say what Danny's talking about?
120	Ashley: Mmm, not really. I'm really confused.
121	[*Danny adds detail to his drawing.*]

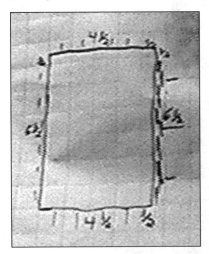

Figure 14. Danny labels the other three "half" units.

~9:00 "I think they're trying to say" . . . half squares and whole squares.

122   [Ms. Sajdak]: Shaina.

123   Shaina: OK. Uhm. On the right-hand side, I think they're trying to say that, uhm, each of the side squares equal a half, and on the other side they all equal a whole, except for the, uhm, t . . . the top and the bottom . . . square on the left—they equal a half. And the other side, the top and the bottom, they equal a quarter.

124   [Ms. Sajdak]: Is that what you're trying to say?

125   Caitlin: Yeah.

126   Danny: I think that that [*top arrow, figure 15*] equals a half and that one, each [*bottom arrow*].

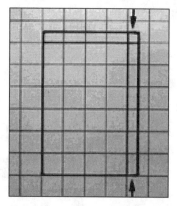

Figure 15. Danny says, "I think that that equals a half (*length at top arrow*) and that one (*bottom arrow*), each."

127   [Ms. Sajdak]: I guess I'm confused as to what you're counting. Because, because, on one side Danny says, "1, 2, 3, 4, 5," [*gestures once more for "6" but doesn't say it*], this . . . and at the top, he's got a half. But on this side [*approaching board*] . . . so Dan, you said that from here to here was one [*measuring sides of units on left edge with fingers, Figure 16-A*].

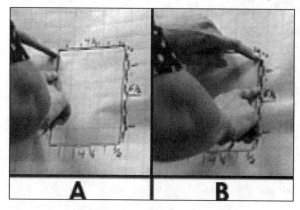

Figure 16. [Ms. Sajdak] marks off Danny's "one unit" on the left of the rectangle (A), comparing it to his "one unit" on the right (B).

128   Danny: Mmm.

129   [Ms. Sajdak]: But on this side [*the right*] you said that from here to HERE is one [*measuring longer distance represented by Danny's marks, Figure 16-B*].

130   Danny: [*very softly and pointing to a spot hidden from view*] That's really one, but . . .

~9:45 "So I'm wondering what you're counting."

131   [Ms. Sajdak]: So I'm wondering what you're counting. Are you counting the ar- . . . are you doing the perimeter, or are you doing the area?

132   Danny: First I started to do the area, but then . . . I started . . .[*unclear*] doing the perimeter.

133   [Ms. Sajdak]: So, so my . . . I'm gonna go back and say that, that we . . . I thought we were doing perimeter.

134   Danny: Yeah.

135   [Ms. Sajdak]: Are you still doing perimeter.?

136   Danny: Yeah.

137   [Ms. Sajdak]: So are you telling me that this side of the rectangle [*the left*] and this side of the rectangle [*the right*] are two different dimensions?

138   Danny: [*shaking head*] No.

139   [Ms. Sajdak]: No.

140   Danny: I messed up on this side [*the right*].

141   [Ms. Sajdak]: You messed up? So how, how . . . how are you . . . So now tell where you are if that's the [*unclear, possibly, "case"*].

~10:30 Caitlin explains Danny's work.

142   Caitlin: OK. Right, here [*pointing to lower right corner*]. . . this side and this side [*right and bottom sides of lower right corner*] equals one half. Like Danny was trying to say. And this side and this half . . . side equals one half [*right and top sides of top right corner*].

143   [Ms. Sajdak]: OK.

144   Caitlin: So when you count it up . . . it's . . . you're counting these . . . this corner as 1 [*upper right-hand corner*]. And then you go down 2, 3 . . . [*counting two at a time down the right side*].

145   [Ms. Sajdak]: OK so, but. So that's what I'm asking you. This is one? [*pointing to length of two half-squares on right side of rectangle*].

146   Caitlin: Yeah.

147   [Ms. Sajdak]: Or is this one? [*pointing to length of one square on left edge of rectangle*].

148   Caitlin: Well what he did, he drew that side [*the left*] as wholes.

149   [Ms. Sajdak]: And this side [*the right*] is not as wholes.

150   Caitlin: Yeah [*nodding*].

151   Danny: I added that and that [*top and bottom right corners, Figure 17-A*] to be . . . one whole and that one . . . these two [*top left and right corners, Figure 17-B*] to be one whole because . . .

152   [*freeze on the diagram*]

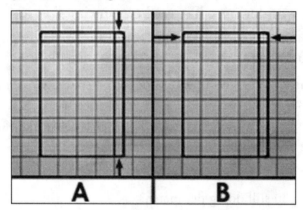

Figure 17. Danny adds the length of the line segments together in A "to be one whole" and does the same for those in B.

153   Danny: . . . they're both a half a . . . a . . . a block. But these ones . . . [*pointing to the four units along the top edge of the rectangle*] they're the full length of the block. So I added them up as wholes. For perimeter.

154   [Ms. Sajdak]: So my qu . . . So, so, Danny, I'm still asking you, I don't know what . . . I, I get confused as to what you're counting. Danae, do you wanna . . . help here?

155   Danae: Yeah.

156   [Ms. Sajdak]: OK.

~11:45 Danae says, ". . . they're trying to do the area more than the perimeter."

157   Danae: Uhm, well, what you might want to do is . . . I think they're trying to do the area more than the perimeter because, even though that that's a half, the line . . . one side . . . If you have a box with four sides, one side of that is a whole. Half, half . . . is . . . IS a half. So . . . [*laughs*] well, it wouldn't be two lines is . . . a whole, it'd be one line is a whole because . . . the AREA is different, but the perimeter . . . is . . . [*softer*] like I have it on here [*holding up her worksheet*].

158   [Ms. Sajdak]: All right. I'm gonna try something different. Let me see if I can . . . [*turning to Danny and Caitlin*]. You can, you wanna, you wanna stay or go?

159   Danny: Stay.

160   Caitlin: Go.

161   [Ms. Sajdak]: Oh. Two different, two different decisions. Danny, you can stay and help me. [*begins drawing*] I want to do a side that's six and a half. And my drawing's going to be enlarged, so it probably won't be perfect. So . . . now, tell me again what we're measuring.

162   [*On the chalkboard, (Ms. Sajdak) draws a rectangle.*]

Figure 18. [Ms. Sajdak]'s $4\frac{1}{2}$ unit × $6\frac{1}{2}$ unit rectangle has half squares along the right and bottom sides.

163   Danny: Four and a half by six and a half.

164   [Ms. Sajdak]: OK. What is four and a half? What do we—when I say, when you're telling me that it's four and a half, what do you mean? What is four and a half?

165   Danny: Like, there's four whole blocks and a half of a . . . whole block.

166   [Ms. Sajdak]: Am I counting blocks?

167   Danny: Yeah . . . squares.

168   [Ms. Sajdak]: Am I? So, all right. So I'm gonna say I'm counting units which are square blocks. So I have 1, 2, 3, 4, 5, 6, and that's a half [*counting squares on left border, then switching to right*].

169   [*(Ms. Sajdak) switches to talking about the right-hand side of her rectangle.*]

170   [Ms. Sajdak]: Can I . . . do th . . . do these two look the same size? [*top two half squares on right, Figure 18*] I know my drawing's a little off.

171   Danny: Yeah.

172   [Ms. Sajdak]: So, so can I put these two together [*the last half-square and quarter-square at bottom right, Figure 18*] and get a half?

173   Danny: Yeah, because . . .

174   [Ms. Sajdak]: Or a whole? Yeah, tell . . . I'm sorry, go ahead.

175   Danny: Yeah . . . 'cause this is a half . . . [*points to last half-square on right, Figure 18*], and that's a half [*points to quarter-square in bottom corner*].

176   [Ms. Sajdak]: How many people agree with Danny? [*no one raises hand*] . . . So what do you want to tell Danny? What's, what's going on? Danny, you pick somebody.

177   Danny: Danae.

~13:45 "Have you changed your mind, Danny?"

178   Danae: Well if you're talking about like his . . . in his picture, the perimeter? With this . . . [*starts to lift her worksheet*]

179   [Ms. Sajdak]: No, we went to . . . we went to area. We did . . .

180   Danae: Yeah, well, and . . .

181   [Ms. Sajdak]: . . . we were counting the blocks.

182   Danae: Yeah. Well, that . . . the square is smaller, so it'd be only one-fourth . . . of . . . It's one-fourth. Because it's a half of the half.

183   [Ms. Sajdak]: OK. So Danny, do you, do you . . . Do you agree with her?

184   Danny: Yeah.

185   [Ms. Sajdak]: Have you changed your mind, Danny?

186   Danny: Yeah.

187   [Ms. Sajdak]: Oh.

188   Danny: . . . now, I think you should count these two, and these two, and those two [*skipping the bottom quarter-square, groups half-squares in twos to top of rectangle*].

189   [Ms. Sajdak]: OK. So Danny . . .

190   Danny: Three . . . it's three wholes.

191   [Ms. Sajdak]: So Dan has changed his mind. So can somebody say what Dan is talking about now. [*softly, addressing Danny*] You pick, Danny, yeah.

~14:30 "That little one there is NOT a whole half . . ."

192   Danny: Uh . . . Nick.

193   Nick: Uhm, now he's, he's changed his mind because now he's figured out that that little one there is NOT a whole half . . . OK.

194   [Ms. Sajdak]: It's not a whole half. [*Students smile, and Nicky nods.*] Absolutely, Nicky.

195   Nick: All right, and . . . now he's saying, uhm, he had 26 before, and now he's adding on three more wholes, so that's . . . equals 29.

196   [Ms. Sajdak]: OK.

197   Nick: Uhm, and so then you could write, twenty-n . . . [*looks at own paper*] twenty-nine and a f . . . and a fourth.

198   [Ms. Sajdak]: Fourth?

199   Nick: Yeah, down there. [*shrugging*] Or a half of a half.

200   [Ms. Sajdak]: This?

201   Nick: Yeah.

202   Danny: If you add . . . that side and that side [*sides of quarter tile in corner*] . . . it equals a half.

203   [Ms. Sajdak]: We're counting blocks, now.

204   Danny: Oh, yeah.

205   [Ms. Sajdak]: We're counting blocks now.

206   Danny: A fourth.

207   [*(Ms. Sajdak) turns toward the class.*]

~15:30 Danny calls on Josh.

208   Danny: Josh . . .

209   Josh: What he's trying to talk about is that he changed his mind, and he, he's gonna . . . put those six . . . those six half tiles . . . are, are gonna be three wholes, altogether.

210   [Ms. Sajdak]: Yep.

211   Josh: But he doesn't know what to do with that, uhm sq . . . uh, square tile. The, the one-fourth of that . . . of, of a whole. Uhm, you just write the, well, altogether what you have except for that one-, uhm, fourth. And then you just add the one-fourth at the end.

212   [Ms. Sajdak]: OK.

~16:00 [Ms. Sajdak] makes a written assignment.

213   [Ms. Sajdak]: This is what I'd like to do, because I want to go on to science. So, so I don't feel like we finished. I would like you to tape an enlarged grid in your journal, and I would like you to solve this problem that I gave you, that we've talked about, in your journal. I want you to find the area and the perimeter, and I want you to tell me in writing how you found the area and the perimeter. I'd like it to be very exact. 'Cause when I'm looking at some of your drawings, I think you could prove they were anything. All right, so I will, I will cut them. You may go back to your seats. It's a wrap. Thanks.

~16:45 The End

Journal articles and papers

Ball, Deborah Loewenberg. 1993. With an eye on the mathematical horizon: Dilemmas of teaching elementary school mathematics. *The Elementary School Journal* 93 (4): 373–397.

Ball provides a powerful account of the challenges and dilemmas of developing a mathematics teaching practice that is responsive to the current reform efforts yet at the same time honors the long-established content of the discipline. Using examples from her own third-grade class, the author examines the types of dilemma that arise in three areas: knowing the mathematical content itself, maintaining respect for children as mathematical thinkers, and creating a community in the classroom.

Ball, Deborah Loewenberg. 1992. Magical hopes: Manipulatives and the reform of math education. *American Educator: The Professional Journal of the American Federation of Teachers* 16 (2): 14–18, 46–47.

Citing examples from her own third-grade mathematics classroom, Ball describes problems that stem from the use of concrete objects or manipulatives (e.g., fraction bars, base ten blocks, and craft sticks) to teach mathematics. The vignettes demonstrate the fallacy of assuming that students will automatically draw the conclusions that their teachers want simply by interacting with particular manipulatives.

Economopoulos, Karen. 1998. What comes next? The mathematics of pattern in kindergarten. *Teaching Children Mathematics* 5 (4): 230–233.

Economopoulos discusses the purposes of developing facility with patterns in kindergarten, explaining that well-designed pattern activities can help children begin to think about such complex mathematical ideas as predictability and consistency. She also points out the connection between such activities in the early grades and the mathematics of later grades.

Goldenberg, E. Paul. 2000. Thinking (and talking) about technology in math classrooms. K–12 Mathematics Curriculum Center Issues Paper Series. Newton, MA: Education Development Center.

Goldenberg proposes some principles to guide decision making about the use of technology in mathematics classrooms. He suggests that decision makers consider the purpose of the lesson and the nature of the thinking being asked of students, then further consider how the genre of technology and the role it plays in the lesson or activity fit with those two essential features of the lesson. Other considerations include what part of the mathematical content of a lesson is of highest priority (and how that is affected by the use of technology) and the extent to which learning the technological tool itself may become part of the goal or a distraction from the goal.

Grant, Catherine Miles. 2000. Beyond just doing it: Making discerning decisions about using electronic graphing tools. *Learning and Leading with Technology* 21 (5): 14–17, 49.

Drawing on a project that incorporates both hand-drawn and computer-generated graphs to enrich second graders' understanding of data and what they represent, Grant notes that the value of electronic graphing tools depends on teachers' recognition of the strengths and limitations of their use in the classroom.

Reitzug, Ulrich C. 1997. Images of principal instructional leadership: From super-vision to collaborative inquiry. *Journal of Curriculum and Supervision* 12 (4): 324–343.

Reitzug examines images of principals' instructional leadership as reflected in ten textbooks on supervision published between 1985 and 1995. His study finds that textbooks have portrayed principals as experts and superiors, teachers as deficient and voiceless, teaching as fixed technology, and supervision as a discrete intervention. Images of professional growth (stressing collegiality and continuous improvement) that are suggested by studies of successful schools differ significantly from these textbook images.

Tracy, Saundra J. 1995. How historical concepts of supervision relate to supervisory practices today. *The Clearing House* 68 (5): 320–325.

Tracy describes seven phases in the evolution of supervisory practice in schools. She looks at each historical phase in relation to its purpose (assisting or assessing), focus, or emphasis; the personnel typically involved; the skills needed to implement supervision; and the assumptions surrounding the process.

Books

Elbow, Peter. 1986. *Embracing contraries: Explorations in learning and teaching.* New York: Oxford University Press.

Elbow argues that what is actually most natural in teaching and learning is a rich messiness of paradox and contradiction. Consequently, he points out, we need to alter our view of how people actually learn and how teachers should teach and grade. In this book, he explores the learning process, the teaching process, the evaluation process, and the nature of inquiry.

Glickman, Carl D., ed. 1992. *Supervision in transition.* Alexandria, VA: Association for Supervision and Curriculum Development.

In this collection of essays (the ASCD 1992 Yearbook), leading scholars in the field of supervision explore the connections between the current changes in school organization and governance structures and the supervisory skills and relationships that are called for by these changes. The collection provides a historical overview of the supervisory process, explorations of promising practices, and consideration of the preparation of teachers. The authors acknowledge the need for supervision to entail professional inquiry and collegiality.

Glickman, Carl D., Stephen P. Gordon, and Jovita M. Ross-Gordon. 1998. *Supervision of instruction: A developmental approach.* Boston: Allyn and Bacon.

This textbook offers a "developmental approach" to the practice of supervision, built on the assumptions that the aim of supervision is to help teachers develop as reflective, autonomous professionals and that supervision itself should ultimately be nondirective. The authors explore a variety of positions, ideas, and practices as well as theoretical grounding and case examples.

Sergiovanni, Thomas J., and Robert J. Starratt. 1993. *Supervision: A redefinition.* 5th ed. Boston: McGraw-Hill.

Sergiovanni and Starratt reconceptualize the supervisory role and its place within the school community. They identify professional and moral authority rather than bureaucratic authority as the central force behind what teachers should do and how supervision should be done. They replace the metaphor of "organization" with one of "community" to describe the nature of schools and schooling. While still emphasizing the importance of traditional supervisory skills and practices, the authors stress the moral relationship that needs to be established between supervisor and teachers for these skills to be exercised wisely.

Videotapes

Mathematical inquiry through video: Tools for professional growth. 1997. A package of videos and teacher professional development materials developed by BBNT Solutions LLC.

This video package presents ten cases of middle-school mathematics classrooms. The videos depict teachers who are working to change their teaching practice according to the NCTM *Standards* and highlight the challenges, ideas, and issues these and other teachers face in this process. Each video is accompanied by a facilitator's guide that includes a description of the video; background information on the school, teacher, and classroom shown in the video; suggested workshop features with video-related mathematical and pedagogical issues and activities; and a complete transcript of the video. For more information on this series, contact Fadia Harik at harik@attbi.com or fadia.harik@umb.edu.

Mathematics: Assessing understanding. 1993. A series of videotapes for staff development. Created by Marilyn Burns. White Plains, NY: Cuisenaire.

This series, with three videotapes and an accompanying teacher's discussion guide, shows a collection of individual assessments of mathematical understanding with students ages 7 through 12. All of the assessments address students' ability to estimate, reason numerically, and compute in problem-solving situations. The one-on-one interviews model for teachers the kinds of questions that are useful for gaining insights into how students are thinking and what they understand. Mathematical topics included are number sense and the place-value structure of our number system, estimation, numerical reasoning, and computation with whole numbers and fractions.

Relearning to teach arithmetic. 1999. A professional development package developed at TERC by Susan Jo Russell, David A. Smith, Judy Storeygard, and Megan Murray. Four videotapes, two study guides. White Plains, NY: Dale Seymour Publications, an imprint of Pearson Learning Group, a division of Pearson Education, Inc.

This two-part video series provides teachers a structured opportunity to explore the ways children develop facility with the four operations (addition, subtraction, multiplication, and division) and the ways teachers can foster the development of this facility. The first package focuses on addition and subtraction; the second, on multiplication and division. Each package contains two videos and a study guide that outlines six professional development sessions. During each session, teachers view and discuss segments of the tapes and work on related mathematics problems. The series is adaptable to a variety of settings, such as after-school sessions, release-day professional development sessions, or summer staff-development experiences. The materials may also be integrated into a longer course or seminar on the teaching and learning of elementary mathematics.

Talking mathematics. 1996. A professional development resource package developed by TERC, Cambridge, MA. Portsmouth, NH: Heinemann.

This package includes a videotape program, a resource guide for staff developers and university instructors, and a book for teachers who are interested in supporting talk and mathematical inquiry in their classrooms. The goal of the package is to provide teachers and staff developers with resources that can help them cultivate good mathematical discourse. The video program specifically consists of an introductory videotape, four 20-minute videotapes on aspects of children's talk, six short classroom episodes, and a 20-minute summary of a *Talking Mathematics* teacher seminar. The package can be adapted to a variety of professional development settings.

Teaching math video libraries. 1995. A series of videotapes for staff development, produced by WGBH. South Burlington, VT: The Annenberg/CPB Math and Science Collection.

This video series provides visual examples of standards-based teaching and learning. Four libraries are available: K–4, 5–8, 9–12, and a K–12 assessment library. The grade-level libraries each include a set of content-standard videos, a set of process-standard videos, and guidebooks. The assessment library provides case-study videos that examine assessment issues in two different classes and a sequence of vignettes that show a variety of assessment techniques from several classes. This collection of video libraries provides grounded images of what classrooms may look like when teachers are developing their teaching in accordance with the NCTM *Standards.*